Literary Criticism for
New Testament Critics

Literary Criticism for New Testament Critics

by
Norman R. Petersen

Fortress Press
Philadelphia

Library of Congress Cataloging in Publication Data

Petersen, Norman R., 1933-
    Literary criticism for New Testament critics.

    (Guides to Biblical scholarship: New Testament series)
    1. Bible. N.T.—Criticism, interpretation, etc.
I. Title.
BS2361.2.P47   225.6′1   77-15241
ISBN 0-8006-0465-2

6519K77   Printed in the United States of America   1-465

Editor's Foreword

If the difference between historical criticism and literary criticism (or interpretation)—both of which have been dealt with in earlier volumes of this series—were stated most sharply, one could say that the historical critic looks through the text to what it refers or points to and treats the text as evidence for something else, while the literary critic looks at the text for what *it* says in itself by means of the patterning or shaping—the informing—of its content. It would be instructive to have the same scholar, or different ones, interpret the same text, asking first historical questions and then literary ones. Surely different results would emerge. A strictly literary critic considering the secret messiah theme in Mark might conclude that this motif contributes to the text's understanding of how it is possible to grasp the revelation of God. A strictly historical critic might conclude that the messianic secret points to the problem that the author of Mark had in trying to reconcile two interpretations of Jesus, both of which were current in the early church. Or the historical critic might see a reference to how the historical Jesus understood his mission.

Professor Petersen, however, has not chosen to deal with literary and historical criticism in this dichotomous way, and that is all to the good. He has rather sought to show that asking literary questions of biblical texts and dealing with their literary features is necessary if they are properly to be used as historical evidence. He discusses the largely unnoticed *literary* problems in the history of *historical* scholarship and sketches a rationale and method for a literary criticism that will be fruitful for historical investigation. The Gospel of Mark is then interpreted at some length and Luke-Acts, more briefly, in order to show how his literary- and historical-critical principles do in fact intermesh.

Considerably more attention is given to the literary analysis of the New Testament materials than to the historical consequences of

5

the literary findings. It should also be observed that whereas the historical implications flow naturally from the literary conclusions, the relationship that is established between the literary and the historical is not a necessary and exclusive one. That is, the literary criticism that Professor Petersen does might be useful for someone who wants to ask theological, existential, or ethical questions of the texts.

DAN O. VIA, JR.
University of Virginia

Contents

I

Literary Problems in the Historical-Critical Paradigm

Historical criticism is concerned with the value of biblical texts as evidence for reconstructing the history to which they refer or of which they are documents. Partly because the texts refer frequently to historical events, and partly because these events have been of religious significance for most biblical critics, historical criticism has been the dominant mode of academic biblical studies for well over a century. But the long history of historical criticism in biblical studies has also shaped this mode of criticism into an academic tradition, *the historical-critical tradition*. Consisting of a complex of traditional problems, methods, and solutions (hypotheses, theories, and historical reconstructions), this tradition constitutes the fundamental "scientific paradigm" of biblical studies.[1] In his book *The Structure of Scientific Revolutions*,[2] Thomas Kuhn introduced the notion of scientific paradigms in order to describe scientific change—"revolution"—as a change of paradigms. Today the historical-critical paradigm is in a process of potentially revolution-

1. For the history of the tradition see Edgar Krentz, *The Historical-Critical Method* (Philadelphia: Fortress Press, 1975); Werner G. Kümmel, *The New Testament: The History of the Investigation of Its Problems*, trans. S. McLean Gilmour and Howard C. Kee (Nashville: Abingdon Press, 1972); and Hans Joachim Kraus, *Geschichte der historisch-kritischen Erforschung des Alten Testaments*, 2d ed. (Neukirchen: Neukirchener Verlag, 1969). For historical-critical method see the brief handbook by Otto Kaiser and Werner G. Kümmel, *Exegetical Method: A Student's Handbook*, trans. E. V. N. Goetchius (New York: Seabury Press, 1967).

2. Second edition, enlarged; *International Encyclopedia of Unified Science*, vol. 2, no. 2 (Chicago: University of Chicago Press, 1970). See also his "Second Thoughts on Paradigms," in Frederick Suppe, ed., *The Structure of Scientific Theories* (Chicago: University of Illinois Press, 1974), pp. 459–82, with a response by F. Suppe, pp. 483–99, and further discussion on pp. 500–517.

ary change. Kuhn has shown that the signs of paradigmatic revolution are principally the emergence of anomalies in the old paradigm and the promulgation of new paradigms to compete with the old one. In the last decade or so both kinds of sign have appeared with increasing frequency in biblical studies, so that today the future of the historical-critical paradigm is a lively question.[3] At stake, however, is perhaps a more important question concerning the future in biblical studies of the historical *mode* of criticism itself. Because it is immersed in the tradition, there is a danger that the baby (the mode) will be thrown out with the bath water (the tradition).

This book represents a modest attempt to preserve the baby, but also to recycle the bath water, so to speak, by trying to purify it methodologically and theoretically. Literary matters are focal in this endeavor because the most vulnerable aspect of the historical-critical paradigm appears to be its theory of biblical literature, while one of the most persistent challenges to the paradigm is expressed in terms of literary criticism.[4] Historical critics have rightly

3. Krentz, *The Historical-Critical Method*, pp. 55–88, discusses problems that have emerged in the method, and James M. Robinson and Helmut Koester, *Trajectories Through Early Christianity* (Philadelphia: Fortress Press, 1971), address themselves to what they see as a crisis of categories that calls for their dismantling and reassembling. Other scholars have attacked the two-source theory that explains the relations between Matthew, Mark, and Luke (e.g., W. W. Farmer and D. L. Dungan), the hypotheses concerning the chronology of New Testament writings (J. A. T. Robinson), and the historical reconstruction of early Christian religion (M. Smith). New paradigms have appeared under the rubric of structuralism and structuralist literary criticism, especially by Erhardt Güttgemanns, whose polemical study, *Offene Fragen zur Formgeschichte des Evangeliums*, 2d improved ed. (Munich: Chr. Kaiser Verlag, 1971), is complemented by his constructive alternative of a "generative poetics" and "linguistic theology," essays on which have been translated by W. G. Doty in *Semeia* 6 (1976). See also Dan O. Via, Jr., *Kerygma and Comedy in the New Testament* (Philadelphia: Fortress Press, 1975), and for French structuralist biblical studies Daniel Patte, *What Is Structural Exegesis?* (Philadelphia: Fortress Press, 1976). For ongoing work in these areas see the journals *Linguistica Biblica* and *Semeia*. In connection with Mark's Gospel, see Norman Perrin's call for a new literary criticism in his essay "The Interpretation of Mark," *Interpretation* 30 (1976): 115–24.
4. Besides the works of Güttgemanns, Via, and Patte cited in n. 3, see also David Robertson, "Literature, the Bible as," in *The Interpreter's Dictionary of the Bible, Supplementary Volume* (Nashville: Abingdon Press, 1976), pp. 547–51, with bibliography; idem, *The Old Testament and the Literary Critic* (Philadelphia: Fortress Press, 1977); and William A. Beardslee, *Literary Criticism of the New Testament* (Philadelphia: Fortress Press, 1970). It should be noted that for most historical critics "literary criticism" refers to *source* criticism! Otherwise the adjective "literary" is used principally in connection with the notion of literary history, which refers to the history of the form and style of the material used in the composition of biblical writings. As a result of this usage, biblical critics have until recently lacked an understanding of literature like that found among literary critics. For the latter see,

concluded that biblical writings are not literary because they do not conform to ancient canons of literature, but at the same time they have wrongly dismissed literary criticism, overlooking the simple fact that the analysis of narrative and verse is not limited by aesthetic canons or values. Whether or not the biblical writings conform to the ancient canons of literature, they do share features with literary texts and are, therefore, amenable to literary criticism. Therefore my concern is to lay some groundwork for a literary criticism that will stand in the service of the historical criticism of biblical texts. For practical reasons I will limit my focus to two narrative texts in the New Testament, the Gospel According to Mark and the two-volume work comprised of the Gospel According to Luke and the book of The Acts of the Apostles (hereafter, Luke-Acts). The remainder of this chapter is devoted to literary problems in the historical-critical paradigm; Chapter II seeks a literary-critical model for the historical criticism of biblical texts; and the last two chapters contain case studies of Mark and Luke-Acts.

THE HISTORICAL-CRITICAL THEORY
OF BIBLICAL LITERATURE

Since others have devoted whole volumes to the historical-critical paradigm, we can focus our attention on what I am somewhat gratuitously calling its theory of biblical literature. The attribution is gratuitous because historical critics do not self-consciously speak of such a theory and therefore have not specifically written about it. Nonetheless, it exists and can be seen in various of its aspects in the writings of the founding fathers, of their students, and of those who survey the whole tradition or its parts, like source criticism, form criticism, and redaction criticism.[5] From such writings I want to reconstruct the theory so that we can see its vulnerable points.

Essential to the historical-critical theory of biblical literature is the evolutionary model upon which it is constructed. An evolu-

---

e.g., René Wellek, "Literature and Its Cognates," *The Dictionary of the History of Ideas*, vol. 3 (New York: Charles Scribner's Sons, 1973), pp. 81–89, and Chapter II, below.

5. Besides the works listed in n. 1, see such studies of specific aspects of the paradigm as Joachim Rohde's *Rediscovering the Teaching of the Evangelists* (Philadelphia: Westminster Press, 1968) on redaction criticism, and Klaus Koch's *The Growth of the Biblical Tradition: The Form Critical Method* (New York: Charles Scribner's Sons, 1969). These and other aspects are dealt with in the several volumes of Fortress Press's series Guides to Biblical Scholarship, edited by Gene M. Tucker (OT) and Dan O. Via, Jr. (NT). See also Güttgemanns, *Offene Fragen zur Formgeschichte des Evangeliums.*

tionary model requires at least four components: (1) something which evolves; (2) sequential stages through which it evolves; (3) a source of power residing in it and by which its evolution is motivated; and (4) an environment in relation to which the thing evolves by adaptation. Form criticism is the principal contributor to the historical-critical theory because it supplies all four of these components.

First, form criticism identified the thing that evolves as the individual preliterary traditions underlying most biblical writings. Second, the beginning and end stages in the evolutionary process were supplied by distinguishing between the earliest stage of originally independent traditional units (e.g., individual sayings, stories, or laws) and the latest stage of their sequential arrangement which appears in the biblical texts as we now see them (e.g., the Gospel of Mark and the book of Genesis). The end stage was thus viewed as a collection (Gunkel, et al.) of traditions, perhaps with intermediate stages of oral or smaller written collections that served as sources for the final texts. In this way source criticism was integrated into the model, as was the earlier notion of literary history, which now pertains to the evolutionary history of the originally traditional units. And finally, the genres of the final texts were determined by the genre(s) of the traditions contained in them—legal traditions formed law books, songs formed song books, and visions formed visionary books or apocalypses. Third, the source of power that led to the terminal texts and their genres was variously located either in the form or the content of the traditions, or in both, since form and content were often seen to be inextricably interrelated. While people did the collecting, they were believed to have responded to forces of form and content that were inherent in the traditions and recognized by the religious communities. Thus legal traditions *attracted* one another to produce lawbooks, and so on. Although this notion was introduced in the early decades of this century by Gunkel, Dibelius, and Bultmann, it is still productive today. In a recent collection of essays by Helmut Koester and James M. Robinson, *Trajectories Through Early Christianity*, the power component, as well as the entire model, is used to show how different formal types (genres) of Jesus traditions led to the formation of generically different Gospels. Sayings of Jesus led to the formation of collections of sayings generically identifiable as "sayings of the wise," as in the hypothetical Q source believed to have been used by Matthew and Luke along with their Markan source, and as in the Gnostic gospel of Thomas. Miracle stories, in turn, led to collections of the same now found in Mark and in John, but also to generically identifiable "aretalogies," which may also have been used by Mark and John (so M. Smith).[6] So, too, revelations like those in Mark 13 led to revelatory or apocalyptic "gospels" in later orthodox and heretical writings (e.g., the Epistle of the Apostles and the Apocryphon of John), while community rules led to the formation of generic "manuals of discipline" (so Robinson, citing the Qumran Community Rule, the Christian "Didache" and the Gospel According to Matthew). And last but not least, taking up a much older idea and placing it within the evolutionary model, Koester argues anew that kerygmatic traditions, that is, those oriented to the death and resurrection of Jesus (see 1 Cor. 15:3–5), led to the formation of a passion narrative (a story about Jesus' death and resurrection) and then to Mark's Gospel, which is seen to contain a collection of traditions that serve to introduce the passion narrative. And because Matthew and Luke apparently used Mark as a source, Koester concludes that they too are generically "gospels." While each of these evolutionary processes is associated with the generic *form* of the traditions (sayings, miracle stories, revelations, etc.), Koester also shows how their christological content contributed to the processes. Thus there is a certain power to the ideas of Jesus as a teacher, miracle worker, revealer, lawgiver, or dying and rising religious hero, and this power is bound up with the corresponding traditional genres. The fourth component, namely, the environment to which the traditions must adapt, is for form critics the religious community. This environment is viewed both sociologically and culturally. Sociologically the community is the bearer of the traditions that must adapt to its needs. Because these needs were believed to be sociologically institutionalized in forms of worship, preaching, teaching, and controversy, form criticism has also been called a sociological method, and one reason for emphasizing this is that it prevents the formal concerns of form critics from being construed as aesthetic concerns. For form critics the genres of early Christian communication were pragmatic sociological media, not art forms. Thus, together with the location of power for evolution in the traditions, the sociological environment also effec-

6. See Morton Smith, "Prolegomena to a Discussion of Aretalogies, Divine Men, the Gospels and Jesus," *Journal of Biblical Literature* 90 (1971): 174–99; and Howard C. Kee, "Aretalogy and Gospel," *Journal of Biblical Literature* 92 (1973): 402–22.

tively ruled out any possibility for creative authorship. The final texts were in every sense communal, collective products, and their genres were the product of the evolution of generically different kinds of traditions. On the cultural side of the environmental component, finally, form critics integrated into their model and into their theory what is called the history-of-religions (*religionsgeschichtliche*) component of the historical-critical tradition. Simply, the history of ancient religions provided the wider environment to which both the traditions and the communities had to adapt.[7]

As elegant as this evolutionary model is, it nevertheless proves to be the most vulnerable aspect of the historical-critical theory of literature because at two points its vulnerability is of such magnitude as to invalidate the model. And because the model is the backbone of the theory, as the model goes so goes the theory. The two critical points are the roles of authors and of genres in the final compositions. In order to get at these points while at the same time preserving as much as possible from the traditional paradigm as a whole, let us consider the relationship between the evolutionary theory produced by the model and another aspect of the historical-critical paradigm, namely, the conclusions of historical-critical *analysis*.

To explain how texts and genres were formed, the evolutionary theory first reverses the process that historical critics followed in *analyzing* the evidential strata in our present texts, and then substitutes for the analytical process the power component of the evolutionary model. That is, historical analysis moves from the present, written text back to the hypothetical earlier stages, while the evolutionary theory posits a development from the earlier stages to the present, written text. The theory therefore inverts the process of analysis, redefines it as an evolutionary process, and reads the evidential strata as evolutionary stages. Once we see how this transformation works we are in a position to separate the conclusions of historical-critical analysis from the evolutionary model that serves to integrate the conclusions in the form of an evolutionary theory. And once we have separated the analytical conclusions from the explanatory theory we are in a position to test both the theory and the conclusions. In this way we may also be able to preserve the conclusions while rejecting the theory. The diagram in Figure 1 forms a basis for reflection. In parentheses beneath each

7. On the history-of-religions component of the paradigm see Kümmel, *The New Testament*, pp. 206–324, 342–62.

14

analytical stage examples related to our case studies are cited. The sequence of examples presumes that the text we are looking at is Luke's Gospel, and through it to the strata of material discovered within it.

FIGURE 1

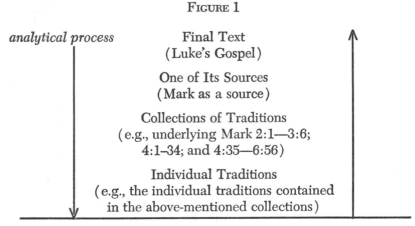

analytical process   Final Text
(Luke's Gospel)

One of Its Sources
(Mark as a source)

Collections of Traditions
(e.g., underlying Mark 2:1—3:6;
4:1-34; and 4:35—6:56)

Individual Traditions
(e.g., the individual traditions contained
in the above-mentioned collections)

"Events"   *evolutionary process*
(i.e., referred to in the narrative
traditions or implied by sayings traditions)

In connection with the analytical process we need to add two analytical principles that are also fundamental to the historical-critical paradigm: (1) every text is first and foremost evidence for the circumstances in and for which it was composed, and in this respect texts serve as documentary *evidence for the time of writing*; (2) seek the earliest and best *evidence for the events referred to in the text*. Together, these two principles require that the historical critic distinguish between two different evidential dimensions of texts. As we shall see, the failure to be consistent in paying respect to this requirement has contributed to the current crisis in the historical-critical theory of biblical literature. But before we deal with the failure we should also recognize the consensus resulting from the application of the principles.

While attending to the first principle, scholars discovered that our present texts frequently contain other texts, that is, as sources, at which point the second principle came into effect on the assumption that sources are earlier and better evidence for the events referred to in the present texts. Thus source criticism and then form

15

criticism made it possible to penetrate the final texts by revealing their written and/or oral sources. At the same time, however, the first principle applies to these new "texts," for they are also evidence for the times when they were written. And so the analytical process resulted in the evidential stages of our diagram. In spite of disagreements about particular source theories and about some of the conclusions drawn by form critics, there is today virtually universal agreement that the stages in our diagram reflect the *history*, for example, of the Jesus traditions—that the individual traditions are the earliest and best evidence for Jesus and that these traditions have had a history whose stages are represented in the diagram. This is not to say, however, that this history was, technically speaking, an evolutionary process. While many believe it was, all that need be said as a result of the analytical process is that textual analysis has discovered in, for example, Gospel writings, a sequence of stages through which their material has passed. On the basis of this consensus we can now proceed to look at the significance of the application of the two principles for the problems of authorship and genre.

In the creative stages of source and form criticism during the first three decades of this century, the first principle was neglected in favor of the second. The search for the earliest and best evidence for the historical Jesus led to the progressive neglect of stages later than that of the individual traditions, the work of Rudolf Bultmann on the synoptic tradition being an excellent illustration of this point. His concentration on the oral development of the Jesus traditions, as seen in *The History of the Synoptic Tradition*,[8] on the one hand culminated in his literary conclusion that the final Gospel writings were but collections and editions of traditions, of groups of them, or of sources, and on the other hand it produced a book on the historical Jesus, *Jesus and the Word*,[9] which was based on what he believed to be the earliest traditional evidence. Then, in his two-volume *Theology of the New Testament*,[10] he reconstructed the history of Christian thought reflected in the history of the Gospel *traditions*, in pre-Pauline traditions, in Paul, and in the Johannine

8. Trans. John Marsh (New York: Harper & Row, 1963).
9. Trans. Louise Pettibone Smith and Erminie Huntress Lantero (New York: Charles Scribner's Sons, 1958).
10. Trans. Kendrick Grobel, 2 vols. (New York: Charles Scribner's Sons, 1951, 1955). While also devoting considerable attention to Paul and John, Bultmann's comments on the writers of the synoptic Gospels appear in vol. 2, pp. 116–18, 120–27, 142–43.

writings, but with a very few words indeed about the theology of the synoptic Gospel writers. In fact, alongside the conclusion that the Gospels themselves were virtually the accidental end-products of communal processes of preservation and transmission, Bultmann viewed the theologies of the Gospels as largely the theologies of the Gospel writers' communities. Compositionally and theologically, authors were but collectors and editors who formally presented their communities' traditions and ideas. Bultmann even denied any generic identity to Gospel writings by viewing the notion "gospel" as a dogmatic rather than literary category, although on this point most of his colleagues still maintained that "gospel" as a generic category was a Christian literary creation. Be this as it may, in form, content, and authorship the synoptic Gospels were seen to be communal products, pervaded by the power of the content of the traditions as were the communities that collected and preserved them. Thus far in the history of research, therefore, the quest for the earliest and best evidence for the events referred to in our texts resulted in a vastly diminished concern for the evidential value of the final texts themselves. But before this situation could be set right, the evolutionary model established itself and brought an end to creative historical-critical research, at least in Gospel studies, until mid-century.

It was at the mid-century mark that the flaws in the evolutionary theory first began to be recognized by the leaders of the historical-critical tradition. Under the banner first of redaction criticism and then of composition criticism,[11] historical criticism returned to the first principle of its analytical paradigm for a second look at the texts themselves as evidence for the time of writing, rather than as evidence for the events referred to. Redaction critics addressed their attention to the final texts and their authors, and in the process reopened the question of the genres of the texts. But while initially thinking of their task as one of taking up unfinished form-critical business, their conclusions have in fact revealed fundamental flaws

11. See Rohde, *Rediscovering the Teaching of the Evangelists*, and Norman Perrin, *What Is Redaction Criticism?* (Philadelphia: Fortress Press, 1969). The substitution of "composition" for "redaction" was made by Ernst Haenchen, *Der Weg Jesu*, 2d ed. (Berlin: DeGruyter, 1968), p. 24, in order to overcome the image of an editor with scissors and paste suggested by the notion of redaction. He thought that "composition" better represents the literary and theological foci of redaction critics. I have retained the term redaction because by whatever name it is identified, redaction criticism is methodologically bound to the evidence revealed by differences between a text and its sources, be they oral traditions or written texts. "Composition" only obscures this bondage.

in the evolutionary theory. Collective authorship has been flatly rejected, leading to new investigations into both the poetics or art of Gospel composition and the intentionality of Gospel writers. And in the course of realizing that individual texts are not merely evolutionary products of the Jesus tradition, it has also been seen that the genres of these texts are not the evolutionary products of this tradition either, since almost all of them antedate that tradition and existed independently of it (e.g., historiography, manual of discipline, testament, apocalypse, aretalogy, sayings of the wise, etc.). Indeed, depending on how one views the genre(s) of Gospel writings, all genres represented in the New Testament are probably general cultural media. While conscious of all these conclusions, however, redaction critics are rarely conscious of the consequences of their conclusions for the historical-critical evolutionary theory, possibly because the theory itself is not one about which there is much self-consciousness. Nevertheless, *the evolutionary theory has collapsed because redaction criticism has pulled the plug on its source of power.* Whereas the theory saw the power of literary formation in a romantic symbiosis of tradition and environment, redaction criticism has relocated this power in authors on the one hand and in genres on the other, with genres now construed as cultural media of communication. Wittingly or not, therefore, redaction criticism has made possible the asking of literary questions about our nonliterary writings. Indeed, I suspect that it has made it impossible not to ask them, since outside of biblical studies issues of authorship, composition, and genre are considered to be literary issues.

But redaction criticism is not literary criticism, and it has yet to realize how passage from the one mode to the other might be effected. For this reason I think it necessary to recognize that redaction criticism cannot answer the questions it has raised without becoming something else, namely, literary criticism. Redaction criticism is, in this respect, a victim both of its disciplinary ancestry and of its own designs.

From their predecessors redaction critics inherited the source-critical conclusion that biblical texts are frequently redactions of sources. But they have turned the assumptions of source criticism upside down. Whereas source critics assume the integrity of our present texts and see verbal and conceptual inconsistencies in them as traces of their sources, redaction critics assume that our texts are composed out of sources and that redactional handiwork is to be seen in verbal and conceptual consistencies that appear throughout the text and across its several sources. For example, because Mark's narrative is composed of originally unconnected individual traditions and perhaps of several small collections of the traditions, wording, style, and themes that appear throughout the text must be redactional additions to the originally unconnected traditions, especially when such elements appear in the present connections between the traditions. The connections are redactional additions to the unconnected traditional sources. Whereas source critics saw their problem in terms of finding sources in Mark, redaction critics see their problem in terms of finding Mark. Thus the compositional integrity of Mark is not something the redaction critic begins with. Rather, it is the very thing he is trying to discover. Rightly or wrongly, the redaction critic is less comfortable with the physically integral text we have before us than with the hypothetical sources he has to reconstruct from it.

Sources surely require us to think about how they have been redacted, but the shift of analytical focus from the literary whole to the preliterary parts has had the effect of dissolving the whole. At best, the redaction critic's view of the whole, as long as it remains redaction critical, is comprised of the sum of redactional devices and effects attributable to authors. Moreover, by basing their method on the distinction between redaction and tradition, redaction critics are forced to look *through* the text by focusing on the relations between it and its sources. For this reason they cannot look *at* the text in order to see, for example, how the units in its linear sequence are related to one another to form the whole. Having cast off the evolutionary model, they nevertheless remain bound to the genetic sequence of stages in textual formation by construing texts as *windows* opening on the preliterary history of their parts rather than as *mirrors* on whose surfaces we find self-contained worlds.[12] Positively, redaction criticism raises the very real problem of having to determine the author's investment in each word, sentence, and unit taken over from his sources. Negatively, however, its methodological and theoretical orientation requires us to focus on something other than the text itself. Redaction criticism's concern for composition and authors thus leads to literary problems that it is not designed to deal with.

12. The metaphors of window and mirror come from the literary critic Murray Krieger, *A Window to Criticism* (Princeton: Princeton University Press, 1964), pp. 3–4.

Redaction critics are victims of their own designs because they also seek to find the integrity of a text in the theological motivation for its redaction. Their expressed goal has been to recover the theology of the evangelists from their redaction of their sources, and in this respect they have also moved beyond the evolutionary theory by attributing the theology of redactions to individuals rather than to communities. In itself the theological goal is not particularly objectionable, but when seen as one of the twin foci of redaction criticism it becomes clear that redaction criticism is not designed to answer the literary questions it has raised. To use an analogy, source and form criticism knocked our textual Humpty Dumpty off the wall and failed to reconstitute him with their evolutionary theory, since the latter produced only an anonymous community product, not Humpty Dumpty. Redaction criticism, on the other hand, has attempted to reconstruct from the seams between the fragmented pieces not Humpty Dumpty but his theology! Redaction criticism has raised what must be called literary questions, but in the last analysis its self-assigned task only contributes to what Hans Frei has called the "eclipse of biblical narrative."

THE ECLIPSE OF BIBLICAL NARRATIVE

In its quest for the earliest and best evidence for events referred to in biblical narrative, historical criticism defaulted on its own first principle, which holds that a text is first and foremost evidence for the time of writing. Redaction criticism sought to remedy this situation and in its failure showed that literary issues are bound up with the first principle: The text itself must be comprehended in its own terms before we can ask of what it is evidence, whether in relation to the time of writing or in relation to the events referred to in it. In connection with the referential focus of the second principle, Hans Frei has identified a hermeneutical problem which complements the broadly poetic, that is, compositional, problems we have been considering. To extend Murray Krieger's happy distinction between the metaphors of mirror and window, if the poetic problem is raised by wrongly looking through a narrative as though it were a window on the evidential stages of its prehistory, the hermeneutical problem is raised by wrongly looking through the narrative window and seeing the events it refers to as its meaning. In Frei's terms, the history-likeness or literal meaning of biblical narrative has been confused with its "ostensive" reference to actual historical events, and the meaning of the history-likeness has been reduced to the meaning of the events. As a result, the narrative shape and meaning of biblical texts have been eclipsed by the significance attributed to the events.[13]

The history of research concerned with Mark's narrative may serve as a useful illustration of Frei's point. At the end of the last century and early in this one, Mark's narrative was viewed as biography, as referring to a sequence of events in Jesus' life and to his own consciousness about his role. The meaning of the narrative was therefore located in the events to which it referred. Jesus did and thought what is reported in the narrative, and what Mark "meant" was the things he reported. From Frei's perspective this historicizing of the narrative confused Jesus the narrative actor and his relations with other actors with Jesus the man and his relations with other men, thus missing what Mark was saying about him by plotting the narrative as he did. The narrative "world" created by Mark was eclipsed by the real-world events envisioned when his narrative was construed as a window on the real world. But by overlooking the first principle the eclipse also led to the sidestepping of the second principle, for together the *two* principles of historical criticism define the referential problem as one of determining the evidential value of the narrative for reconstructing the events to which it refers. In this light, the literary character of Mark's narrative must be understood before its evidential value can be assessed. Literary criticism would thus be either a fundamental stage of historical criticism or a stage which in this respect must precede historical criticism.

Historical critics are sure to be offended by this conclusion, since according to their paradigm the work of William Wrede and Karl Ludwig Schmidt[14] demolished the historicizing error by showing that Mark's narrative was not a historical or biographical report. In this they are in agreement with Frei and are undoubtedly right. But historical critics will also say that Wrede and Schmidt obviated

---

13. Hans Frei, *The Eclipse of Biblical Narrative: A Study in Eighteenth and Nineteenth Century Hermeneutics* (New Haven, Conn.: Yale University Press, 1974).
14. William Wrede, *The Messianic Secret*, trans. J. C. G. Greig (Greenwood, S.C.: Attic Press, 1971); originally published in 1901. Karl Ludwig Schmidt, *Der Rahmen der Geschichte Jesu* (Darmstadt: Wissenschaftliche Buchgesellschaft, 1964); originally published in 1919. The interpretation of Wrede and Schmidt by Bultmann is as much a part of the historical-critical tradition as their own work. See Bultmann, *History of the Synoptic Tradition*, pp. 1–7 and 338–50; the latter section contains the most extensive reportage of Schmidt's argument to be found in English.

Frei's literary concerns by showing that Mark was so dependent on traditional sources (Schmidt) and traditional ideas (Wrede) as to have had little or no authorial control over his narrative. For the historical critic there is therefore no true narrative or narrative "world" attributable to Mark, no real poetic (compositional) activity detectable in his collection, and only a theological intent that is more or less an expression of communal beliefs. Thus the historian's problem is to deal either with the evidential value of Mark's traditional material (à la form criticism), again viewed referentially, by the way, or with the theological significance of his editing of the material (à la redaction criticism). At this point we come back to the problems we dealt with in considering the evolutionary theory, only now in a more concrete form vis-à-vis a specific text. Here it is necessary to see that the historical-critical appeal to Wrede and Schmidt in rejecting a literary approach to Mark's narrative overlooks the literary issues Wrede and Schmidt did not examine.

Above all else Wrede and Schmidt were polemicists against historicizing interpretations of Mark's narrative. They did not constructively set out to explore literary aspects of the narrative. Thus Wrede showed that traces of Jesus' alleged messianic self-consciousness in Mark were dogmatically informed ideas that had developed only after the time of Jesus. These later ideas are preserved in Mark's narrative as themes and are therefore not evidence for Jesus' self-consciousness. But Wrede did not set out to explore the literary implications of these themes, since for his polemical purposes it was only necessary for him to show that they did not originate with Jesus. Consequently, the literary implications of these themes remain to be explored in specifically literary terms. Schmidt's concern was equally historical but with equally literary side effects. He saw his task as one of showing that the sequence of episodes in Mark's narrative did not represent a corresponding historical sequence of events in Jesus' life. By comparing Matthew, Mark, and Luke, Schmidt was able to demonstrate that each Gospel differed most from the others in the links between narrative units rather than in the units themselves. Schmidt concluded that these were traditional units which, like pearls on a string, were juxtaposed by being placed in a linear sequence that created the impression of historical sequence. For Schmidt, this impression was virtually the accidental result of Mark's collecting of the traditions. But his conclusion also implies that the impression of a historical sequence was not the intentional result of Mark's designs as a narrator, in which case we cannot properly speak of Mark's collection as a narrative, of a narrative world represented by it, or of Mark as a narrator! He is a collector and the text he put together was a collection, not a narration! Against the historicizers Schmidt succeeded in demonstrating that the narrative "world" created by the juxtaposition of traditions does not correspond to the real world of Jesus. While his point was made by showing the artificial linkage of the traditions, Schmidt did not seriously consider the literary implications of *the impression of narrative* created by the sequence of units in Mark; nor did he reflect on the surprising coherence of Mark's narrative world.[15] Thus the so-called themes, the problem of compositional integrity and segmentation, and the narrative world of Mark are all literary issues that need to be explored before we can fulfill our responsibilities to the first principle of historical criticism.

Wrede, Schmidt, and their redaction critical successors have produced evidence that makes our task more difficult than that of the extrabiblical literary critic. Because they have shown, for example, that Mark's narrative is not a completely free authorial creation, we cannot assume that Mark has a conscious investment in every word, sentence, and unit we find in his narrative, as we could if we were reading a novel. But while Mark was not a completely free narrator, redaction critics have made it equally clear that he was not completely dependent either. In going beyond redaction criticism to literary criticism we will therefore have to find new ways to discern his freedom. In light of the questions not asked by Wrede, Schmidt, et al., we can at least ask the open question of how the text of Mark works to create the impression of being a narrative. To ask this question, however, we have to know something about how narrative in general usually works, and it is at this point that the biblical critic has to suspend source and redaction critical operations and begin to think like a literary critic.

Our own next question, therefore, has to do with the ways literary critics think about texts.

---

15. The most thorough consideration of this problem is by Jürgen Roloff, "Das Markusevangelium als Geschichtsdarstellung," *Evangelische Theologie* 27 (1969): 73–93.

II

A Literary-Critical Model for Historical Critics

Texts as windows, texts as mirrors, or texts as both. Murray Krieger, a literary critic, uses these metaphors to characterize the main stages in the modern history of literary-critical thinking. Nineteenth- and early-twentieth-century critics thought about texts as though they were windows to meaning that lay beyond them, but against this the Anglo-American New Criticism and similar movements in other countries in the early decades of this century rebelled by construing texts as mirrors within which meaning was locked up. Krieger, however, is one among many critics who today deny the sharp alternatives posed by the two metaphors and insist that we must see "the mirrors as windows too," for literature both traps us in the looking glass and takes us through it.[1]

Behind these metaphors is a literary-critical history that instructively parallels the history of biblical criticism. The metaphor of windows corresponds to a historical-critical stage shared by both disciplines. The metaphor of mirrors, on the other hand, corresponds to a stage literary critics have already passed through, while biblical critics are just on the verge of entering it. Consequently, at a time when literary critics are seeking to secure a more balanced bifocal vision, biblical critics are beginning to become aware of the mirrorlike aspect of biblical texts. The parallel histories of the two disciplines therefore suggest that biblical students can learn from their literary colleagues as long as they remember to distinguish between the metaphors and the stages they represent, and as long as they remember that they are victims of an academic

---

1. Murray Krieger, *A Window to Criticism* (Princeton: Princeton University Press, 1964), pp. 3–70. For current discussion see the journal *New Literary History*.

cultural lag. The lesson of literary-critical history is twofold: it teaches us that our current problems are those of the New Critics and related movements like the French *explication de textes,* the Russian Formalists, and the Prague Structuralists;[2] but it also teaches us that we cannot ignore our apparently inevitable return to a bifocal approach to our texts. If we learn our lessons well, we will not once again suffer from cultural lag by absolutizing the metaphor of mirrors as we did the metaphor of windows. Having considered in Chapter I some of the things biblical critics saw in looking through their textual windows, let us begin our search for a literary-critical model by reflecting on literary criticism's shift from windows to mirrors.

THE REVOLT AGAINST HISTORICAL CRITICISM

From the eighteenth century on, both literary and biblical studies were dominated by historical or otherwise causal (genetic) approaches to the interpretation of the written word. But by the nineteenth century, historical method itself had become identified with an ideology known as historism or historicism. Exceeding the legitimate historical-critical tasks of establishing and interpreting the written word as evidence, historicism reduced the possible meaning of such evidence to what it meant and construed what it meant as the product of its immediate historical and cultural context, of which authors were more or less representatives. In this way the spirit of the culture became the primary perspective from which its products could be construed. As the understanding of texts became a matter of understanding the culture that produced them, the critic increasingly worked from the cultural context to the text rather than vice versa, as historical method requires. To be sure, extratextual information about language, style, and concepts is necessary for understanding texts, but to the degree that emphasis is placed on explaining them from such information, the text itself loses control over the interpretive process. And this was what happened to the historical criticism of the nineteenth century. But what was not so clear at the time was the difference between historical method and historicistic interpretation. Because historicism

2. See René Wellek and Austin Warren, *Theory of Literature,* rev. ed. (New York: Harcourt, Brace & World, 1956), pp. 139–41; René Wellek, "Literary Criticism," *The Dictionary of the History of Ideas,* vol. 1 (New York: Charles Scribner's Sons, 1968), pp. 596–607; and idem, *Concepts of Criticism* (New Haven, Conn.: Yale University Press, 1963).

shifted its focus from the historical method's fixation on the text-as-evidence to the culture that "caused" it, historicism is in fact an aberrational by-product of the method. The difference was not appreciated at the beginning of this century when a number of academic disciplines, including the biblical and the literary, revolted against historicism, and not infrequently against the historical method with which it had become identified.[3]

From the perspective of intellectual history the multifronted revolution was not only against the causal or genetic explanation of things but it was also in favor of systemic explanations. Because genetic explanation had obscured the perception of effects by reducing them to their causes, the effects became the focus of the revolutionaries' attention. The effects came to be viewed as self-contained and self-regulated systems, or as parts of such systems, and the functional relations of parts to wholes came to replace the relationship between cause and effect.[4] In literary studies the critic thus became concerned with the things of which a text was "made," with how they "worked" to make the text what it was or appeared to be, and with what literary works essentially "were," that is, ontologically.[5] Individual texts were seen to form closed systems (cf. Krieger's "mirrors"), while also participating as parts in the wider system of texts called "literature." And so along with the close reading and formalistic study of individual texts, we find a related concern with the "literariness" of literature and with "poetics" as theory of literature, that is, of how literature is "made," "poetics" being derived from the Greek verb *poiein,* meaning "to make." But poetic "making" is not the causal activity extrinsic to the literary work; it is rather the systematic operations intrinsic to the work

3. On historicism see: Georg G. Iggers, "Historicism," *The Dictionary of the History of Ideas,* vol. 2 (1973), pp. 456–64; René Wellek, "Literary Theory, Criticism, and History," in *Concepts of Criticism,* pp. 1–20; Wellek and Warren, *Theory of Literature,* pp. 38–45, 73–135; William K. Wimsatt, Jr., and Cleanth Brooks, *Literary Criticism: A Short History* (New York: Knopf, 1957), pp. 522–51; and Hans Frei, *The Eclipse of Biblical Narrative: A Study in Eighteenth and Nineteenth Century Hermeneutics* (New Haven: Yale University Press, 1974), index, s.v. "historicism."
4. See Jean Piaget, *Structuralism,* trans. Chaninah Maschler (New York: Harper & Row, 1970). Note that Piaget's definition of structure is broader than that, for example, of Lévi-Strauss. Piaget is really referring to underlying systems not logical structures.
5. Besides the references in n. 2, see Wellek and Warren, *Theory of Literature,* pp. 142–57, on "The Mode of Existence of a Literary Work of Art"; and Roman Ingarden, *The Literary Work of Art,* trans. George G. Grabowicz (Evanston, Ill.: Northwestern University Press, 1973).

itself. Thus the literary work, and by extension literature itself, came to be viewed as an autonomous system.[6]

Strangely enough, in biblical studies the revolt against historicism took the form of theological hermeneutics rather than of poetics. Concerned with the principles of understanding and of interpretation, the hermeneutical revolution associated with the introduction of existential phenomenology by Karl Barth and Rudolf Bultmann became separated from poetic questions because it focused on the content rather than on the composition of biblical texts. Biblical students, whose interests were as much theological as historical, now distinguished between the study of the theological things referred to in the texts (*Sachkritik*, which is at best poorly translated as "object criticism"; better therefore to think of theological criticism) and historical criticism, to which matters of textual poetics were relegated. As a result, historical and "object" criticism have been in constant tension with one another ever since, with the tension being located in the problematic nature of their relationship. In Krister Stendahl's terms, the problem is one of determining how one moves from what a text *meant*, which is the subject of historical criticism, to what it *means*, which is the subject of theological hermeneutics ("object" criticism).[7] For our purposes this interesting and important problem is less significant than the consequences of the distinction between hermeneutics and poetics. Although biblical students do not usually speak of poetics, we have seen that they deal with poetic matters. We have seen, too, that these poetic matters were relegated to historical criticism and therefore came to be taken up into historical criticism's evolutionary theory of biblical literature. What we have not seen is that the distinction between hermeneutics and poetics, and the hermeneutical revolt against historicism, left poetic matters to the historicistic explanations of the evolutionary theory. Even the polemics of Wrede and Schmidt against the historicizing interpretations of Mark's narrative remained

---

6. The next step beyond the notion of the autonomy of the work of art concerns the multiple meanings ("polyvalency") of the work, on which see *Semeia* 9 (1977), ed. John Dominic Crossan: *Polyvalent Narration*.

7. Krister Stendahl, "Biblical Theology, Contemporary," in *The Interpreter's Dictionary of the Bible, A–D* (Nashville: Abingdon Press, 1962), pp. 418–32. See also Otto Kaiser and Werner G. Kümmel, *Exegetical Method: A Student's Handbook*, trans. E. V. N. Goetchius (New York: Seabury Press, 1967), pp. 35–37; and for the hermeneutical revolution see James M. Robinson and John B. Cobb, Jr., *New Frontiers in Theology, Volume 2: The New Hermeneutic* (New York: Harper & Row, 1964), esp. pp. 1–77, 164–97, 198–218.

within the historicist camp by explaining the text of Mark as the product of its context.

The historicist character of biblical poetics is evident when we see that current problems in biblical poetics are ones that literary critics revolted against decades ago. For example, René Wellek, a major historian of international literary criticism, has described how the nineteenth-century orientation to the extratextual circumstances in which literature was produced resulted in "a lack of clarity on questions of poetics" and in "the astonishing helplessness of most scholars when confronted with the task of actually analyzing a work of art."[8] These results sound very much like the complaints expressed today by many biblical students about themselves and their colleagues. For this reason it is important for biblical students to consider seriously the literary-critical revolt against historicism. Unencumbered by the separation of poetics from hermeneutics, literary critics proceeded from a new set of working assumptions, perhaps the most important of which concerned the autonomy of texts as analytical objects: "the meaning of a work of art is not exhausted by, or even equivalent to, its intention [understood as a cause]. As a system of values, it leads an independent life [i.e., it constitutes a "world" separate from the real world in which it was produced]. The total meaning of a work of art can not be defined merely in terms of its meaning for the author and his contemporaries."[9] According to Krieger's metaphor of mirrors, the work is like "an enclosed set of endlessly faceted mirrors ever multiplying its maze of reflections but finally shut up within itself."[10] Meaning is "locked" into this maze.

Remembering the lesson of Krieger's historical characterization, however, a concluding comment is called for about the rebellion against historicism. While we surely cannot forget the specter of historicism and the reductionist genetic fallacy toward which it tends, we should beware of perpetuating the nineteenth-century confusion of historicism with historical method by rejecting historical method along with historicism. As long as we have texts we will have the challenge of reconstructing history from them, and historical method is the only rational means by which we can do so. The problem is to be a historian without being a historicist.

8. Wellek and Warren, *Theory of Literature*, p. 139.
9. Ibid., p. 42.
10. *A Window to Criticism*, p. 3.

HISTORICAL CRITICISM WITHOUT HISTORICISM

Despite their rebellion against historicism and historical method, literary critics have not been without respect for historical concerns. This is abundantly evident not only from the current rebels against the New Criticism but also from earlier rebels against the old criticism like René Wellek and Austin Warren, whose classic handbook of literary method and theory, *Theory of Literature*, proposes a division of critical labors in which historical criticism retains an important position. Although their divisions are not uncontroversial, by making some adjustments in them we can secure a general orientation to the kinds of literary-critical things biblical critics might do. The principal categories they suggest are those around which their book is structured: the preliminary task of ordering and establishing evidence; *intrinsic* studies of literature; and *extrinsic* approaches to the study of literature.

Their first category is important because it is the only one of the three that falls entirely within the traditional domain of historical criticism, as the notion of "evidence" in their rubric already implies, and because it refers to forms of criticism that are applicable to all texts, whether literary or not. In fact, the applicability of this category to biblical texts is confirmed by the authors when to describe it they borrow a distinction developed in biblical studies! Like biblical students they distinguish between a "lower" criticism concerned with "the assembling and preparing of a text," which in biblical studies is called text criticism, and a "higher" criticism concerned with "the problems of chronology, authenticity, authorship, collaboration, revision, and the like,"[11] which in biblical studies includes source criticism. In biblical studies, however, higher criticism includes consideration of poetic matters (composition; genre) and of content (the message of the text as distinct from its "meaning").[12] Therefore, while the ordering and establishing of evidence may be preliminary to other forms of criticism, or to other stages of historical or literary criticism, it is not *precritical* activity as Wellek and Warren suggest.[13] What these other forms or stages of criticism

11. Wellek and Warren, *Theory of Literature*, p. 57.
12. See, for example, the historical-critical introductory handbooks of Otto Eissfeldt, *The Old Testament*, trans. Peter R. Ackroyd (New York: Harper & Row, 1965); and Werner G. Kümmel, *Introduction to the New Testament*, trans. Howard C. Kee, rev. Eng. ed. (Nashville: Abingdon Press, 1975).
13. A judgment already expressed by the literary critic David Daiches, *Critical Approaches to Literature* (New York: W. W. Norton & Co., 1956), p. 328 (cf. pp. 321–39); for further comments see E. D. Hirsch, Jr., *Validity in*

are is further illuminated by the authors' distinction between intrinsic and extrinsic criticism, which also raises some new issues.

The issues surrounding the distinction between intrinsic and extrinsic derive from the two different ways in which it is used. In one it refers merely to the difference between the intrinsic and extrinsic study of individual texts, in which case, for example, the question of composition would be an intrinsic matter because it concerns the poetics of the individual work, and that of genre extrinsic because it involves the analysis of other texts also, or of other things, namely, genres, which are not texts. In the second and more common New Critical understanding of the distinction represented by Wellek and Warren, intrinsic criticism is the study of literary texts in the context of a corpus called "literature," whereas extrinsic criticism is the study of literary texts or of literature from some non-literary perspective such as sociology, psychology, and the history of ideas. In this context both composition and genre are the concerns of intrinsic criticism, since the concept of genre is intrinsic to the study of literature. The problem of this double usage, however, is not whether genre is an intrinsic or extrinsic concern, for generic criticism is not disallowed either way. The problem is rather that the second use makes claims about the nature of literature and literary criticism that result in the exclusion of some works from the corpus of literature, thereby denying the applicability to them of literary criticism. While the first use of the distinction between intrinsic and extrinsic literary criticism is merely text-centered in its focus ("ergocentric"), the second requires a prior distinction between literary and nonliterary works because it sees literary criticism as the relating of a literary work to other literary works. To make this distinction we need to know what makes a verbal text literary or nonliterary.

With their introduction of a literary approach to literature, the revolutionaries began a lengthy and still-continuing debate over the nature of literature. The debate centers on the question of whether criteria for differentiating between literary and nonliterary works can be found in distinctively literary uses of language. Those who argue for an essential linguistic difference claim that there are linguistic universals by which the difference can be established. For example, some say that literary language is more expressive and

Interpretation (New Haven: Yale University Press, 1967), esp. pp. 127–63. See also Wellek, "The Term and Concept of Literary Criticism," in *Concepts of Criticism*, pp. 21–36.

pragmatic than scientific language, and more deliberate than everyday language. But those who argue against such differential features have thus far been able to provide nonliterary examples for every feature the essentialists have come up with.[14] As a result, owing to a lack of evidence for the essentialist position it seems wisest to conclude with many literary critics that the label of "literature" is arbitrarily attributed to verbal works by cultures or by critics on the basis of their own values rather than of universal essences. In the words of one such critic, E. D. Hirsch, Jr.:

> By claiming to be intrinsic to the nature of literature, it ["aesthetic criticism"] implies that the nature of literature is aesthetic. But, in fact, literature has no independent essence, aesthetic or otherwise. It is an arbitrary classification of linguistic works which do not exhibit common distinctive traits, and which cannot be defined as Aristotelian species. Aesthetic categories are intrinsic to aesthetic *inquiries*, but not to the nature of literary works.[15]

Recognizing the arbitrary nature of the notion of literature, we must revert to the first use of the distinction between intrinsic and extrinsic criticism. Intrinsic criticism, which we have already seen to be a necessary part of the activity involved in establishing a text, will now focus on the individual text, and it will do so in the manner suggested in Chapter I, and by Hirsch, namely, by drawing on the categories of literary critics. Extrinsic criticism, on the other hand, will include all the extrinsic approaches listed by Wellek and Warren, but also others like the Bible and literature, historical reconstruction, theological criticism, and so on. In all cases extrinsic criticism will consist of relating the individual text, or features of it, to other texts or to extratextual concerns, and in all cases it will presuppose intrinsic criticism.

Once we so thoroughly redefine Wellek's and Warren's three divisions it becomes apparent that the divisions cannot be as neatly separated from one another as they would have us believe. The preliminary stage is no longer precritical because intrinsic criticism is necessary to perceive the composition and message of a text and

---

14. See, e.g., Wellek and Warren, "The Nature of Literature," *Theory of Literature*, pp. 20–28; *New Literary History* 5, no. 1 (1973), devoted to the question "What is literature?"; and *New Literary History* 4, no. 1 (1972), on "The Language of Literature." See also n. 15, below.

15. E. D. Hirsch, Jr., "Some Aims of Criticism," in Frank Brady et al., eds., *Literary Theory and Structure* (New Haven: Yale University Press, 1973), pp. 41–62; quotation from p. 52. See in the same volume an essentialist argument by Monroe C. Beardsley, "The Concept of Literature," pp. 23–39.

because "the problems of chronology, authenticity, [and] authorship," and also of genre, require textually extrinsic considerations pertaining to textual features. In biblical studies the ordering and establishing of evidence is the end product of historical and literary criticism as applied to such evidential problems. For the historical critic, literary criticism is therefore a means to historical-critical ends. On the other hand, once these higher critical problems have been attended to, even if only in a preliminary way, strictly intrinsic and extrinsic concerns can be entertained in studies specifically devoted to them, for example, to the composition of individual texts or to generic relations between them, or to sociological, psychological, or intellectual-historical aspects of them. Literary criticism may also be an end in itself. Yet in all these cases the results of intrinsic and extrinsic criticism will feed back into the fund of higher critical knowledge, although they may also point beyond it as in recent studies of the Bible as literature.

What, then, are the specific issues entailed in intrinsic and extrinsic criticism? Wellek and Warren devote their handbook to the traditional forms of such criticism, but because their book was designed to deal with problems in a disciplinary context other than the biblical, I would like to consider an analytical model that encompasses most of the several critical tasks associated with their notions of intrinsic and extrinsic criticism. The model I have in mind confirms the impression gained from Wellek and Warren, among others, namely, that it is possible to do literary criticism in the historical study of biblical texts without being historicistic. Several models exist, but of those I am familiar with one seems best suited to our needs—the modified communications model introduced to literary critics with some success by Roman Jakobson.[16] Every model is in some respects inadequate, but Jakobson's offers the best

16. Roman Jakobson, "Linguistics and Poetics," in Thomas A. Sebeok, ed., *Style in Language* (Cambridge, Mass.: Technology Press, 1960), pp. 350–77. See the response by René Wellek in the same volume, pp. 414–18. I. A. Richards, "Functions of and Factors in Language," *Journal of Literary Semantics* 1 (1972): 25–40. Other models are Karl Bühler's linguistic model, *Sprachtheorie* (Jena, 1934), which Jakobson assimilates to his own; M. H. Abrams' model for literary theories, *The Mirror and the Lamp* (New York: W. W. Norton & Co., 1958), esp. pp. 6–29; and Paul Hernadi's expansion of Jakobson's model, "Literary Theory: A Compass for Critics," *Critical Inquiry* 3 (1976): 369–86. Hernadi's essay is as important for understanding current critical movements as Abrams' book is for the past. On models and their uses see, e.g., Colin M. Turbayne, *The Myth of Metaphor*, rev. ed. (Columbia, S.C.: University of South Carolina Press, 1970); and Philip Pettit, *The Concept of Structuralism: A Critical Analysis* (Berkeley and Los Angeles: University of California Press, 1975), pp. 100–18.

formal controls for isolating textual information that the historian can use as empirical evidence, including evidence for the poetic and referential functions of verbal texts, which are two critical issues facing the historical critic of biblical texts. The communications model will therefore serve to replace the evolutionary model of earlier biblical historical criticism.

ROMAN JAKOBSON'S COMMUNICATIONS MODEL

Although Jakobson's model stands on its own, it is useful to see its dependence on three sources: Karl Bühler's model of the expressive functions of verbal communications—the emotive, the conative, and the referential; a communications model comprised of senders, receivers, messages, channels and codes; and his own firsthand experience as a linguist who was a major figure in two fronts of the literary-critical revolution referred to earlier, those of the Russian Formalists and the Prague Structuralists, both of which were concerned with the poetic functions of language.

Of these dependencies the one that calls for immediate clarification is the last because in recent decades both Jakobson and these movements have been associated with the phenomenon called structuralism. The association is historically correct, but it is necessary to observe the difference between Russian Formalist, Prague Structuralist, and Jakobsonian intrinsic literary concerns and the extrinsic concerns that the structuralist par excellence, Claude Lévi-Strauss, has with regard to literature and to texts in general. The necessity is all the more important because Jakobson introduced Lévi-Strauss to structural phonology and to Formalist narrative analysis, both of which have been developed by Lévi-Strauss into what is commonly understood today as "structuralism,"[17] and because Jakobson has also co-authored an article with Lévi-Strauss and frequently praises his ideas. My concern here is merely to distinguish between the intrinsic orientation of the communications model and the extrinsic orientation of Lévi-Strauss's structuralism. That the former is related to the latter in what is called semiotics, the study of signs, is a matter beyond discussion in this context.[18]

The basis for the distinction I am suggesting derives from Lévi-Strauss's distinction between empirical and logical structures, which

17. See especially Pettit, *Concept of Structuralism*; and Jonathan Culler, *Structuralist Poetics* (Ithaca, N.Y.: Cornell University Press, 1975).
18. See Umberto Eco, *A Theory of Semiotics* (Bloomington, Ind.: Indiana University Press, 1976), for full discussion and literature.

formally parallel Noam Chomsky's surface and deep structures. Simply, Jakobson's *communications model* is designed to reveal features of surface structure, whereas Lévi-Strauss employs another model, a *transformational model*, to discover the deep, logical structures underlying empirical phenomena and to identify the transformations by which these deep structures assume various empirical forms.[19] Formally speaking, redaction criticism is also based on a transformational model in the sense that its task is to show the transformations (redaction) by which text A (a source) becomes text B (the final text). In Lévi-Strauss's structuralism, however, texts are construed as transformations of logical rather than textual structures. What is more, although his structural analyses can tell us about empirical or historical relations, Lévi-Strauss insists that structural analysis is dependent upon the prior ordering and establishing of the empirical evidence. Therefore, because he approaches texts from the perspective of extratextual structures, and because he presupposes that intrinsic criticism has already been undertaken with regard to the texts he uses, his approach is in every way extrinsic. Jakobson's communications model, on the other hand, serves fundamentally intrinsic concerns while at the same time providing evidential windows opening out on extrinsic horizons. The transformational model assists Lévi-Strauss in comparing numerous texts and in relating them to logical structures. The communications model enables Jakobson to unravel the structure of intrinsic functions that constitute individual verbal utterances.

The relationship between intrinsic and extrinsic in Jakobson's model is based on his parallel distinction between the *factors* and *functions* operative in verbal communications. The factors are extrinsic to actual communications because they define the a priori conditions for every verbal communication. The functions correspond to the factors but are empirically observable features in-

---

19. Lévi-Strauss's model is most accessible in his parallel disputes with A. R. Radcliffe-Brown over the notion of social structure and with V. I. Propp over the notions of form and structure in folkloric narrative. On the former see "Social Structure," in Claude Lévi-Strauss, *Structural Anthropology*, trans. Claire Jacobson and Brooke Schoepf (New York: Basic Books, 1963), pp. 277–323, and a "postscript," pp. 324–45; see also Hugo G. Nutini, "Some Considerations on the Nature of Social Structure and Model Building," in E. Nelson Hayes and Tanya Hayes, *Claude Lévi-Strauss: The Anthropologist as Hero* (Cambridge, Mass.: M.I.T. Press, 1970), pp. 70–107. On the latter, see Lévi-Strauss, "Structure and Form: Reflections on a Work by Vladimir Propp," and "Structuralism and Literary Criticism," in Claude Lévi-Strauss, *Structural Anthropology, Volume Two*, trans. Monique Layton (New York: Basic Books, 1976), pp. 115–45, 274–76. For Propp's illuminating response see n. 33, below.

trinsic to actual communications. They are recognizable by the ways in which they orient communications, or aspects of them, to one or more of the factors. The beauty of the model from the historian's perspective is that the a priori factors lead us to look for the corresponding verbal functions in texts, which in turn provide information we can use as evidence for those factors that are *actually* involved in individual texts. The a priori model thus leads us to intrinsic criticism, which provides evidence upon which extrinsic criticism can also be performed. The historical critic can approach any text and ask: what elements in the text perform functions that are related to the extrinsic, a priori factors and thereby provide evidence about the roles these factors play in the composition of the text?

The communications model requires us to think of our texts as communications. In order to see what this requirement entails, we turn to Jakobson's exposition of the factors and functions:

The ADDRESSER sends a MESSAGE to the ADDRESSEE. To be operative the message requires a CONTEXT referred to ("referent" in another, somewhat ambiguous nomenclature), seizable by the addressee, and either verbal or capable of being verbalized; a CODE fully, or at least partially common to the addresser and addressee (or in other words, to the encoder and decoder of the message); and, finally, a CONTACT, a physical channel and psychological connection between the addresser and addressee, enabling both of them to enter and stay in communication. (P. 353)

Jakobson displays these factors in the following diagram:

CONTEXT

ADDRESSER	MESSAGE	ADDRESSEE
	CONTACT	

CODE

The corresponding functions are represented in a parallel diagram (p. 357):

REFERENTIAL

EMOTIVE	POETIC	CONATIVE
	PHATIC	

METALINGUAL

Before we examine the ways in which this model encompasses intrinsic and extrinsic issues, three points need to be mentioned.

First, Jakobson appears to belong to the essentialist camp because he used this model to reveal what it is that "makes a verbal message

35

a work of art" (p. 350). However, it is clear from his argument that "no text is completely literary or completely non-literary" (Hernadi)[20] because all texts as verbal communications are subject to the several factors and their corresponding functions. Second, messages differ structurally as a result of the hierarchical predominance of one or more functions in their verbal structure and therefore of one or more factors in their communications situation (p. 353).[21] Therefore, not all functions are of equal significance in every message. And third, because Jakobson's comments are cryptically brief, with few references to narrative, and based on messages of sentence length or its equivalent, especially the Formalist views of narrative will help us to supplement his exposition of the functions. For these reasons, too, our own efforts will be tentative and exploratory in nature.

Jakobson begins his exposition of his model with the three linguistic functions proposed by Bühler—the emotive, the conative, and the referential. Bühler related these respectively to the grammatical first person of the addresser, the second person of the addressee, and the third person of someone or something spoken about (p. 355). They also correspond, respectively, to what M. H. Abrams has called expressive, pragmatic, and mimetic theories, although Bühler's functions are intrinsic to messages whereas the theories Abrams refers to are extrinsic approaches to works of art.

Going beyond Bühler's simple identification of *the emotive or expressive function* with the first person singular, Jakobson sees this function as more generally evident in a message's dominant structural orientation to the addresser, and specifically in direct expressions "of the speaker's attitude towards what he is speaking about," regardless of whether his attitude is "true or feigned" (p. 354). Jakobson's example is the linguistic interjection (i.e., exclamatory words, phrases, or sounds), but literarily the emotive function is related to the topic of "point of view" in narrative criticism, where an important distinction is made between the author's point of view, the "implied author's" point of view (Wayne Booth), and the fictive narrator's point of view (cf. Jakobson's qualification, "whether true or feigned").[22] As we will see later, the notion of plot is also re-

20. See Paul Hernadi, "Literary Theory," p. 380.
21. See also Roman Jakobson, "The Dominant," in Ladislav Matejka and Krystyna Pomorska, eds., *Readings in Russian Poetics: Formalist and Structuralist Views* (Cambridge, Mass.: M.I.T. Press, 1971), pp. 82–87. The idea of dominance makes Jakobson a relative essentialist at best.
22. While not exhaustive, the best bibliography and discussion of issues involved in "point of view" is Françoise Van Rossum-Guyon's "Point de vue ou

lated to point of view because the plotting (arrangement) of episodes implies a view of them and of their relations to one another. The emotive function in narrative thus requires consideration of literary-critical reflection on point of view, plot, and what Abrams calls expressive theories of literature. And on the current scene this includes speech-act theory.[23] With the help of this reflection the biblical critic will find criteria for determining the (real or fictive) addresser's attitude toward, or point of view on, what he is speaking about. Once such information has been produced it then becomes evidence for the narrator of the biblical "message," and to some extent of the actual author, depending on how the narrator is related to the actual author in a given text. For example, in the case of pseudonymous writings the implied author is a fictive author whose point of view nevertheless raises historical questions about the actual author.

Again going beyond Bühler's grammatical second person, Jakobson cites the grammatical forms of command, that is, the vocative and the imperative, as expressions of the *conative function,* which orients the message to the addressee. Here, too, however, further criteria for determining textual evidence for the addresser's goals in communicating with the addressee must be sought from literary critics. Besides traditional pragmatic theories and, again, speech-act theory, phenomenological theories oriented to the phenomenology of reading and to the "implied reader" (W. Iser) are useful, as is the protracted debate over what has been called the intentional fallacy, which pertains as much to the emotive function.[24] All these theories and issues need to be reviewed before we can move from the intrinsic conative function to the extrinsic matter of the actual addressees or audiences of biblical texts.

perspective narrative," *Poétique* 4 (1970): 476–97. For more recent contributions related to structuralism and speech-act theory see Seymour Chatman, "The Structure of Narrative Transmission," in Roger Fowler, ed., *Style and Structure in Literature* (Ithaca, N.Y.: Cornell University Press, 1975), pp. 213–57. On earlier "expressive theories" see Abrams, *The Mirror and the Lamp,* p. 21–26.
23. On speech-act theory and literary criticism, see the comments and bibliography in Hernadi, "Literary Theory," and Chatman, "Structure of Narrative Transmission."
24. See n. 23, above; Abrams, *The Mirror and the Lamp,* pp. 14–21; Wolfgang Iser, *The Implied Reader* (Baltimore: Johns Hopkins University Press, 1974); and Robert Detweiler, *Story, Sign, and Self: Phenomenology and Structuralism as Literary-Critical Methods* (Philadelphia: Fortress Press, 1978). On the intentional fallacy see the discussion and literature in Alistair Fowler, "The Selection of Literary Constructs," *New Literary History* 7 (1975): 39–55; Göran Hermerén, "Intention, Communication, and Interpretation," ibid., pp. 57–82; and Hirsch, *Validity in Interpretation,* passim.

Because of the wide-ranging problems entailed in both the emotive and conative functions, these few references to the kinds of things at stake in them will have to suffice for the present. Our brevity should not be taken as a minimizing of the importance of the two functions. They are just less accessible than others.

One of the more accessible functions is the *referential*, which was Bühler's third function. It is also one of the most important for narrative analysis, since narrative is *always* "about" something. In Jakobson's terms the referential function is the one that dominates narrative messages and thereby subordinates the emotive, conative, and other functions to it. Its dominance, however, is also the source of a problem already indicated, for example, in Aristotle's *Poetics*, where he described narrative (*diēgēsis*) as the verbal imitation (*mimēsis*) of actions.[25] M. H. Abrams has shown how from classical to modern times such mimetic theories have explained art "as essentially an imitation of aspects of the universe."[26] The now widely recognized problem posed by such theories is their tendency to confuse the worlds represented by narratives, for example, with the real world, and to interpret narratives in relation to it. The problem has been described in various ways. We have seen it referred to as a historicist extrinsic approach to literature (Wellek and Warren), as viewing texts as windows (Krieger), and as an eclipse of biblical narrative (Frei). But in view of Jakobson's referential function, let us think of it as the "referential fallacy" (Umberto Eco).[27]

The function and the fallacy can best be explained by relating Jakobson's comments on the referential function to his notion of signs.[28] In the essay I have been referring to he mentions signs and objects but does not systematically relate them to his communications model. The diagram in Figure 2 displays the major distinctions from both his theory of signs and his communications model; it will serve as the basis for our discussion of both the referential function and, shortly, of the poetic function.

25. See Gérard Genette, "Boundaries of Narrative," *New Literary History* 8 (1976): 1–13.
26. *The Mirror and the Lamp*, p. 8; cf. pp. 8–14.
27. Eco, *A Theory of Semiotics*, pp. 58–66.
28. Roman Jakobson, *Main Trends in the Science of Language* (New York: Harper & Row, 1974), pp. 11–25. See also Emile Benveniste, *Problems in General Linguistics*, trans. Mary Meek; Miami Linguistics Series, no. 8 (Coral Gables, Fla.: University of Miami Press, 1971), "The Nature of the Linguistic Sign," pp. 43–48. Their updating of Saussure's notion of signs should be used to correct Pettit, *The Concept of Structuralism*, pp. 1–32.

FIGURE 2

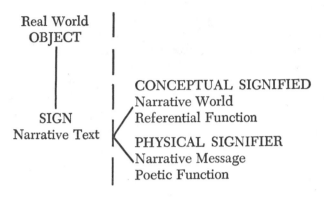

Real World
OBJECT

CONCEPTUAL SIGNIFIED
Narrative World
SIGN — Referential Function
Narrative Text
PHYSICAL SIGNIFIER
Narrative Message
Poetic Function

The two columns in the diagram represent two basic distinctions, one between the sign and object, the other between two aspects of the sign itself, namely, the physical aspect that since de Saussure is technically called the signifier, and the conceptual aspect that is technically called the "signified." For example, the acoustical or graphic image represented by $c/a/t$ is the physical signifier of the conceptual "signified," *cat*, which is to be distinguished from a real live cat that may or may not be referred to by the sign composed of this signifier and its signified (as in the case of a metaphorical cat). In these terms the referential *function* of the signifier $c/a/t$ is to refer the sound or marks to the conceptual "signified," *cat*. The referential *fallacy*, on the other hand, consists of construing the signifier alone as the sign and as referring directly to the real world object without regard for the "signified," for example, a metaphorical cat. Why this is linguistically and semantically fallacious is spelled out by others.[29] For our purposes we can illustrate the fallacy by applying the distinctions associated with signs to narrative, that is, by viewing the narrative text as a sign.

According to Jakobson, the poetic function (see further below) associated with the message factor "deepens the fundamental dichotomy of signs and objects . . . by promoting the palpability of signs" (p. 356). Because the "palpable" aspect of signs has to do with the physical signifier, the poetic function is bound up with it, not with the "signified," which is rather associated with the referential function and the context factor in Jakobson's model. Therefore, while the poetic function deepens the dichotomy be-

29. See, e.g., Eco, *A Theory of Semiotics*, pp. 58–66.

tween sign and object, the referential function minimizes the dichotomy by conceptually denoting, representing, or referring to things. The referential function of language is what logicians call "object language" because it represents objects in conceptual form (p. 356). Alternatively, the referential function consists of propositional content; it is what the message is "about," as long as "about" is understood to be part of the message and not something in the real world outside the message. Now in narrative criticism this referential content is spoken of as the narrative "world," which is the sum of propositions a narrative implies or expresses about its actors and their actions in time and space.[30] Consequently the referential *function* in narrative is to be located in the world created by the narrative, and the referential *fallacy* consists of thinking about this world as though it were a direct representation of the real world, overlooking the conceptual autonomy of the narrative world. Indeed, the fallacy is twofold. It is fallacious literarily because it mistakenly posits a real world where there is only a narrative world, and it is fallacious historically because it assumes what the historian must demonstrate, namely, the evidential value of the narrative world for reconstructing the real world of events to which it refers. To be consistent with the first principle of historical criticism it is necessary to understand the composition of the narrative world as part of a message communicated by an addresser to an addressee (cf. Krieger's "mirror"). To be consistent with the second principle it is necessary to determine how the narrative world is related to the real world which it seems to describe (cf. Krieger's "window").

After the referential function Jakobson goes completely beyond Bühler to deal with three other functions: the phatic, the metalingual, and the poetic. The first properly belongs to the rhetorical axis of communication, the third to the mimetic axis of representation, and the second a little bit to each!

The *phatic function*, which consists of an orientation to the contact factor or channel of communication, for example, texts as such, is the most difficult to relate to narrative. Of this function Jakobson writes: "There are messages primarily serving to establish, to prolong, or to discontinue communication, to check whether the channel works ('Hello, do you hear me?'), to attract the attention of the interlocutor or to confirm his continued attention ('Are you listening?' ...)" (p. 355). What aspects of narrative perform such func-

30. See, e.g., Wellek and Warren, *Theory of Literature*, pp. 212–25, "The Nature and Modes of Narrative Fiction."

tions as these? Titles would appear to provide one example because they signal the opening or closing of the channel, depending on whether they appear at the beginning or end of a text (in ancient texts titles commonly appear at the end). Chapter divisions, too, or their episodic equivalent, may also serve to prolong or otherwise make one conscious of the channel. But possibly of greater significance are the internal means by which narratives begin and end, by which, in Aristotle's terms, the narrative action's beginning is signaled through the introduction of a "complication" (*desis*) and its ending through the presentation of the complication's "resolution" (*lusis; Poetics* 18. 1f. 1455b). In yet other terms,

The beginning is that part which does not of necessity follow any other part but after which another part is present or results as a natural consequence. On the other hand an end is that part which is inevitably or regularly the natural result of another part, but from which no further part results. The middle follows one part, and another part follows it. (*Poetics* 7. 4–6. 1450b)

The only problem reference to Aristotle poses is that his arguments are related to the notion of plot, which in Jakobson's model is related to the poetic rather than the phatic function. Nevertheless, I suspect that plot elements also perform phatic functions to the extent that some of them open and close the channel of narrative communication. In any event, the phatic function is in narrative always subordinate to the referential function.

More obviously relevant to narrative is the *metalingual function* that is oriented to the code(s) in which messages are cast. Language, for example, is an "over-all code" comprised of "interconnected subcodes" (p. 352).[31] These provide speakers with the competence (Chomsky) not only to say anything at all but to say both different things and different kinds of things. The grammar of a (natural) language makes it possible to inflect verbs, decline nouns, make direct statements, ask questions, shift from the active to the passive voice, and so on. By the same token, the shared competence provided by codes makes it possible to decode as well as to encode. Indeed, without codes there could be no speech and therefore no verbal communication. But there are other kinds of codes too: codes of behavior and of dress, of values, of ideas, of customs, and so on. Yet the kind of code that is of equal if not greater significance for the biblical critic is the generic code that makes it possible, for example, to utter parables, proverbs, and riddles, or to

31. On the notion of code see, e.g., Eco, *A Theory of Semiotics*, pp. 36–38, 48–150.

tell fairy tales, write novels, biographies, or history books and, as "addressees," to discern the differences between them, so that we do not confuse a riddle with a question or with a fairy tale. The notion of code refers to the cultural conventions by which meaning is differentiated. Through the metalingual function the textually extrinsic generic code intrinsically contributes to the shaping of the meaning of messages.

Jakobson derives the metalingual category from logicians who, as we have seen, call referential speech, that is, speech about objects, "object language," and speech about language "metalanguage" (p. 356). In applying this category to messages he finds it functioning when interlocutors become self-conscious about the communication of meaning (cf. the phatic self-consciousness about the channel of communication): "Whenever the addresser and/or the addressee need to check up on whether they use the same code, speech is focused on the code: it performs a METALINGUAL (i.e., glossing) function." " 'I don't follow you—what do you mean?' . . . 'Do you know what I mean?' . . . 'I mean . . .' " (p. 356). Examples of this aspect of the metalingual function are found in Mark's Gospel where he explains Aramaic expressions by translating them into Greek, that is, from one linguistic code into another (see Mark 5:41; 7:11, 34; 15:22, 34), or where he explains Jewish practices to his addressees (see Mark 7:3–4; 15:42). Such explanations indicate that Mark and his addressees share Greek codal elements, but not Aramaic, while Mark to some extent shares Aramaic and Jewish codes with others in addition to his addressees.

Jakobson treats the metalingual function as a verbal self-consciousness about code, but he also speaks about the encoding of messages. Because his examples (above) deal with the former and not the latter, we will have to supply them ourselves from sources he has elsewhere approved of. Our concern is with the textually intrinsic functions of extrinsic genres in the process of encoding and decoding.

In biblical studies the question of genre has been taken up by form critics almost solely in connection with smaller oral genres like parables, proverbs, miracle stories, laws, and so on. Folklorists, too, deal with oral genres like these, but also with larger genres like legend, tale, and myth. The literature on genre is as diverse as it is vast.[32] But to be consistent with Jakobson's orientation we need to

32. Some of this literature is referred to in my essay "On the Notion of Genre," *Semeia* 1 (1974): 134–81.

refer to the leading student of genre in the Russian Formalist tradition, V. I. Propp, whose *Morphology of the Folktale* and related essays comprise possibly the most substantial contribution ever made to the study of genre.[33] While biblical form critics construed genre in terms of style and form, and saw them as the products of the sociological situation in which the genre was employed, Propp's morphological approach locates generic traits in the common infrastructure of narratives that on their surface seem to look alike. Starting with a corpus of texts generally perceived as belonging to the same class, Propp discovered that underlying the diversity of actors and actions represented in the texts there is a relatively fixed sequence of certain kinds of actions. He called these kinds of actions "functions," since they operated to maintain the flow of the narrative, and defined the genre of the (Russian) fairy tale in terms of the sequence of functions they all have in common. The number of functions and the kinds of functions, and their sequential relationships, define narrative genres in structural terms.

According to Propp the morphology of genre therefore has to do with the conventions surrounding the selection and combination of functional units, and in this respect the metalingual function of genres approximates Jakobson's poetic function which, as we will see, is also concerned with the arrangement of textual parts. I mention the poetic function here only to show how metalingual generic functions differ from it. For unlike the poetic function, which arranges (plots) the elements of the text's narrative world, the generic pattern of arrangement derives from a generic code that is extrinsic to the text. There are therefore two aspects of arrangement in a narrative; the poetic (i.e., plotting) we usually refer to as compositional, the metalingual or codal we call generic. Both are intrinsic to the text, but the former is recognizable *only* through intrinsic analysis, whereas the latter is recognized only if one knows the extrinsic generic code. And because the generic code of a culture is a system of differences, that is, of genres whose differences signal differences of meaning, it is as difficult as it is necessary to understand the *system* in which a text was encoded. It is difficult if we do not share the system, but difficult even if we do because

33. V. I. Propp, *Morphology of the Folktale*, 2d ed. (Austin, Tex.: University of Texas Press, 1968); idem, "Transformations in Fairy Tales," in Matejka and Pomorska, eds., *Readings in Russian Poetics*, pp. 94–115. An English translation of Propp's response to Lévi-Strauss (see n. 19, above), "Structure and History in the Study of the Fairy Tale," trans. Hugh T. McElwain, will appear in a forthcoming issue of *Semeia* edited by John Dominic Crossan.

we are not always conscious of it, any more than we are conscious of the grammatical system upon which our every utterance depends. It is necessary, on the other hand, because to decode a message we later readers have to know the code employed by the encoder and the decoder, for we as critics are also decoders.

The question of the genre or genres of Gospel writings illustrates the metalingual problem of generic code. The question has yet to be answered to the satisfaction of everybody, but the variety of answers offered is instructive. Some people, for example, argue that "gospel" refers to a unique literary creation of early Christianity. In pointing to the uniqueness of this alleged genre, however, there is a clear tendency to overlook the problem of just how unique a code can be and still be shared, and therefore make communication possible. New genres certainly emerge, but they must do so differentially in relation to other genres in a generic system. To have understood Gospels as belonging to a distinct genre, it would have been necessary for the original addressees to know what it was distinct from, so as to be able to understand Gospels as what they generically were. Consequently, to say that "gospel" is a unique Christian genre only raises the problem of generic code; it does not solve it. Yet other people, however, have seen Gospels as biographies, while others differentiate between them, seeing Mark as an aretalogy, or as related to that genre, or as somehow related to the genre of apocalypse, Matthew as a manual of discipline, and Luke, together with its companion volume, Acts, as history-writing. In all these cases before we can fully understand (decode) these texts we have to identify their generic code in relation to the differential generic system in which they were encoded.

The cooperation of poetic and generic principles of arrangement in the shaping of one and the same text requires a final comment about method. Because poetic principles are discernible only through intrinsic analysis, the search for them constitutes an independent yet preliminary stage of criticism. A second stage devoted to generic principles is dependent upon the first stage for an understanding of the distinctive compositional features of the text in question, but it is also independent since it requires that we extrinsically study other texts that look like the one we are concerned with. This stage entails a search for the infra-structure that underlies the different yet similar texts and accounts for their similarity in structural (not structuralist!) terms. Importantly, in the case of Gospel writtings we must not be led astray by seeing the infra-structure in the common denominator of information about Jesus. On the one hand this information is based on common traditions and even sources (Matthew and Luke apparently used Mark as a source), not on a common generic code, while on the other hand Propp has shown that it is not the *actors* who are the clues to generic structure but both the number and kinds of actions associated with various actors in a class of narratives, and the relatively fixed sequence in which these actions appear. A third stage is then required, one in which the two principles of arrangement operative in the text are compared in order to see the relationship between generic code and poetic composition in it. This stage will reveal the significance of the code for our understanding of the composition.

We come now to the last of Jakobson's functions, the *poetic function*, which Abrams assigns to the concerns of objective theories.[34] Here again Jakobson's use of sentence-length examples requires us to extrapolate from his principles. I want to suggest that in narrative the poetic function corresponds to the notion of plot, and in particular to the notion of plot developed by the Russian Formalists. But before we explore this suggestion let us consider Jakobson's argument.

The poetic function of language is its "focus on the message for its own sake" (p. 356) or, in Fredric Jameson's terms, its "auto-referential" use.[35] Jameson's term is instructive because it differentiates the auto-reference of the poetic function from the conceptual reference of the referential function, and thereby requires us to think again about the two aspects of signs, the signifier and the signified. It will be recalled that Jakobson saw the poetic function as "promoting the palpability of signs" and thereby deepening "the fundamental dichotomy of signs and objects." The poetic function calls attention to the signifier, not to the propositional content it signifies (the referential function), not to the signifier as a channel (the phatic function), and not to the codal form of the signifier (the metalingual function). The poetic function is rather concerned with the arrangement of the signifier's components.

According to Jakobson, *selection* and *combination* are "the two

34. *The Mirror and the Lamp*, pp. 26–29. The "objective" theories correspond to what Wellek and Warren have called intrinsic criticism and to Krieger's metaphor of mirrors; in other words, to the New Criticism and related movements.

35. Fredric Jameson, *The Prison-House of Language: A Critical Account of Structuralism and Russian Formalism* (Princeton, N.J.: Princeton University Press, 1972), p. 202, but also throughout.

basic modes of arrangement used in verbal behavior," and "the poetic function projects the principle of equivalence from the axis of selection into the axis of combination" (p. 358). The axis of combination refers to the linear sequence, for example, of words in an utterance. Jakobson uses as an example the utterance "the horrible Harry." The sequence of these three words comprises the axis of combination. The axis of selection, on the other hand, refers to the field of words the speaker could have used. Since "Harry" is presumably both the conceptual referent and the object (person) whom the utterance is about, the selection of this name did not require much decision. But why, Jakobson asks, the choice of "horrible" when *equivalent* words would have been equally appropriate to the sentiment of the speaker, for example, "dreadful," "terrible," "frightful," "disgusting"? He answers: the selection of "horrible" represents the poetic function, for the principle of equivalence that normally operates in selecting one word from among equivalents here governs the combination of "horrible" and "Harry." The poetic device of paronomasia (wordplay) is reflected in the combination of equivalent sounds, "horri-" and "Harry." This combination of equivalent sounds deepens the dichotomy between the sign (the utterance) and its object (Harry) by referring the addressee to the palpable signifier— not to its conceptually referential "signified" (Harry is horrible), not to the channel, not to the code, and not to the addresser or addressee (pp. 357–58).

Poetic verse is the most conspicuous source of devices reflecting the "poetic" use of equivalence as a principle of combination or arrangement, as is evident in the fundamental principle of *parallelism* that governs the selection and arrangement of items (sounds, words, syntax) both within and between parallel lines (pp. 358ff.). But parallelism also reflects, if I may, the equivalent notion of *repetition*. All three terms—equivalence and its sub-forms of parallelism and repetition—point to traits of the poetic function. The last two terms, however, point beyond verse to narrative prose, enabling the biblical student to recognize the poetic function, for example, in the five formally parallel discourses of Matthew's Gospel, in the parallelisms between Luke's Gospel and Acts and between individual stories and discourses associated with the heroes of Luke-Acts, and in the triadic complexes surrounding the three passion predictions in Mark 8:27—10:52. Thus there is prima facie evidence for supposing the validity of exploring the poetic function in these texts. Such an exploration must begin by seeking the intrinsic devices that perform the function of calling attention to the arrangement of narrative units of which the texts are comprised. The principles of equivalence, parallelism, and repetition provide clues to these devices.

The poetic function has yet another dimension in narrative, one which the Russian Formalists expressed in terms of a distinction between story and plot.[36] In what follows I will suggest that their notion of story corresponds to Jakobson's referential function, to the conceptual "signified" of sign theory, and to the narrative "world" of which literary critics speak, while the Formalist's notion of plot corresponds to Jakobson's poetic function, to the physical "signifier" of sign theory, and to the notion of plot in some literary criticism.

For the Russian Formalists the referential function is encompassed in the notion of *fabula*, a story or "story-stuff." Empirically, this "story-stuff" consists of the total world of events (i.e., actions of actors) either described or referred to in a narrative—but in their causal sequence or temporal order regardless of the order in which they appear in the narrative. Independently of events in the real world, should the narrative be biographical or historiographical, and independently of sources a writer may have used, the sum of events described or referred to constitutes the autonomous world (signified) of that narrative (signifier). From *this* world the writer selects and combines events for his own purposes. For the Formalists, the process of selection and combination produces the plotted narrative. "Plot" (*sujet*) thus refers to the order of events and their relations as seen in the narrative (signifier) while methodologically plot *devices* are identified by contrasting the sequence of events in the narrative world of story-stuff with the sequence of incidents in the narrative itself. Plot devices call attention to themselves when the narrative differs from its narrative world, as for example in the device of the flashback, where at one point in the narrative an event is referred to that took place before the point in time at which the narrative began. The flashback is but one example that the poetic function in narrative need not always be based on the principle of equivalence.

Finally, besides giving us new insights into the empirical rela-

---

36. Besides the critical accounts by Culler and Jameson, see the essays in Matejka and Pomorska, eds., *Readings in Russian Poetics*, especially Boris Ejxenbaum's "The Theory of the Formal Method," pp. 3–37; Lee T. Lemon and Marion J. Reis, eds. and trans., *Russian Formalist Criticism: Four Essays* (Lincoln, Neb.: University of Nebraska Press, 1965); and Stephen Bann and John E. Bowlt, eds., *Russian Formalism: A Collection of Articles and Texts in Translation* (New York: Barnes & Noble, 1973).

tionship between the referential and poetic functions, the Formalist understanding of plot also involves the emotive function. Their notion of plot corresponds to the general notion of plot, but also to "plot as mediated through 'point of view' . . . ,"[37] for the author/narrator's attitude about what he is narrating is indicated by the motives he introduces as links between incidents. He does not merely say that one event took place after another, but that one took place because of another. So, for example, Mark tells a story about the feeding of the five thousand (6:30–44) and another about Jesus walking on the water (6:45–52), and concludes that the disciples did not understand what was happening in the second story because they had not understood what had happened in the first. And as is abundantly evident from reading Luke's Gospel in a Gospel Parallels, where one can see how Matthew and Mark tell the same stories, Luke repeatedly introduces causal and motivational links between stories that are baldly separate from one another in the other Gospels, creating thereby not only new literary units but also motivations for their sequential relations.

CONCLUSION

In the following chapters I want to explore principally the referential and poetic functions. Our consideration of Mark's narrative (Chapter III) is oriented to a demonstration that it is a plotted narrative, contrary to the conclusions of Wrede, Schmidt, and Bultmann. In Chapter III we will therefore entertain literary considerations and conclude by showing how they define the historical question of this narrative's evidential value for the time of writing. In our second case study we will proceed differently in order to see other dimensions of a biblical literary criticism. Chapter IV is therefore concerned with the evidential value of Luke's two-volume narrative for reconstructing some of the events to which it refers. In both case studies our task is to isolate literary evidence bearing on historical questions and to point to the kinds of answers the evidence suggests. No attempt will be made to answer these questions fully, for to do so would take us well beyond the scope of the present essay.

37. Wellek and Warren, *Theory of Literature*, p. 218.

III

Story Time and Plotted Time
in Mark's Narrative

The first two chapters have contributed both a problem and a possibility to our exploration of the poetics of Mark's narrative. In its most radical terms the problem is this: Due to Mark's extensive use of preshaped material, the impression that his book is a narrative may be an illusion, the accidental product of the juxtaposition of his material (cf. Chapter I). The possibility, on the other hand, is that despite the use of sources the product before us may create a self-coherently intelligible world[1] that displays traces of its having been plotted. Taken together, *this* illusion of reality (the conceptual "signified") and its plotted form (the physical signifier) would define Mark's book as a narrative (cf. Chapter II). Our task is to determine whether the possibility is an actuality and, if it is, what it might tell us about Mark's narrative message and the occasion for which it was composed. If it is an actuality we will be able to prove that the impression of narrative is not an illusion without denying the claim that Mark was excessively dependent upon preshaped material.[2] And positively, because our proof is comprised of poetic evidence it will provide us with a literary basis for understanding the narrative as a message.

Employing the notion of plot developed in the preceding chapter, I want to examine Mark's plotting of incidents from his narrative world onto the axis of incidents in his narrated message. It will be recalled that the narrative world is comprised of all events described

---

1. See René Wellek and Austin Warren, *Theory of Literature*, rev. ed. (New York: Harcourt, Brace & World, 1956), p. 214, and ch. 16, passim.
2. Methodologically, extensive lapses in coherence will falsify my argument. If minor, however, they become the subject of source, redaction, and even text-critical analysis.

or referred to in the narrative, but in their causal and logical sequence, whereas the plotting of this world is to be seen in the ways its components have been selected and arranged in a sequence of narrated incidents. These ways are plot devices. Thus the narrative world and the, narrated incidents comprise two levels of information that are related through plot devices. Because the levels each have their own temporal sequence, we can focus our attention on the plotting of the temporal coordinates of Mark's narrative world, using them as a means of access to his plotting of the actions of his actors. Narrative being a time art in which writers orchestrate their reader's experience by relating story time, plotted time, and reading time, we will begin at the beginning of Mark and work through his book by commenting as we go on the orchestration of these three temporal features. Ideally, the best way to do this would be to use a roll of shelf paper on which to record the narrative "score" from beginning to end. But since we are bound to prose and pages, we will instead have to pause from time to time to see where we have been and where the narrative is leading us.[3]

MARK 1:1–15: THE INTRODUCTION OF
TEMPORAL COORDINATES

The first thirteen to fifteen verses of Mark's text are often considered to be introductory to the entire book. Although chapters and verses are not original to the text, having been added hundreds of years later to facilitate reference to it, we can use them for purposes of reference as long as we remember that the internal definition and arrangement of parts is a matter of composition and, perhaps, of plotting. Some of the reasons for isolating 1:1–13/15 as a section will be seen in our observations about it; others will be seen in our consideration of what follows it.

One distinctive feature of this section is that its temporal references introduce the fundamental temporal coordinates of Mark's narrative world as a whole. The first coordinates are found in verses 2–3, which refer to a prophecy that the narrator attributes to

3. Because the following discussion is in the form of a literary-critical commentary, I will assume that the reader will be reading the commentary with the text of Mark at hand. The translation employed is the Revised Standard Version. For practical reasons, reference to secondary literature will not be made. General bibliography and discussion of other approaches may be found in Werner G. Kümmel, *Introduction to the New Testament*, trans. Howard C. Kee, rev. Eng. ed. (Nashville: Abingdon Press, 1975). The most relevant recent works on Mark are those by E. Trocmé, T. J. Weeden, W. Kelber, and H. C. Kee.

Isaiah, although it begins with elements found in Malachi, not Isaiah! Errors aside, the reference establishes two coordinates, the first being the implied time of Isaiah's issuing of the prophecy, which is indeterminately located in a time prior to that of the very first episode in the narrative, and the second a time when his prophecy would be fulfilled—a time when a messenger would come to cry *in the wilderness* for people to prepare the way of the Lord. This prediction appears to be fulfilled in 1:4–8, where we find that John the baptizer appeared *in the wilderness*, preaching repentance and baptizing. John's appearance and activity constitute another coordinate which is also the first plotted incident in the narrative, even though it is cast in summary form to embrace what he did over an extended period of time. At the end of the summary, however, we find other coordinates when we learn that besides preaching repentance and baptizing John also predicted one or more future events—the coming of someone after him who would be mightier than he, someone who would baptize with the Holy Spirit. Immediately following this prediction, we find yet another coordinate in the second plotted incident in the narrative, and also another actor, Jesus. In 1:9–11 we learn that he came to John and was baptized by him, and that in the course of his baptism Jesus (alone) saw the Spirit descend upon him and heard a heavenly voice declare to him that he was its beloved Son. Then in 1:12–13 a further incident is plotted as Jesus is said to have been driven into the wilderness by the Spirit and for a period of forty days to have been tempted by Satan and ministered to by angels. Next, we learn in 1:14–15 of two more incidents: that John was arrested, and that Jesus went into Galilee where, over an unspecified period of time, he preached the gospel of God, saying, "The time is fulfilled, and the kingdom of God is at hand; repent, and believe in the gospel." Since John is not again an actor in the plotted narrative, which henceforth is focused on Jesus, Jesus' appearance on the scene of plotted incidents constitutes at least a partial fulfillment of John's prediction since Jesus' baptizing with the Holy Spirit is yet to come. But let us also observe that like the Baptist, Jesus no sooner appears in the plotted sequence of incidents than *he* implicitly predicts a future moment in which the kingdom, at that time only "at hand," would come. This prediction introduces the last coordinate in 1:1–15.

Let us pause and reflect on the several coordinates of 1:1–15 and on how only some of them have been plotted in the narrative. On the level of story time we have a temporal continuum that begins with the indeterminate time when Isaiah prophesied and ends with the equally indeterminate time of the coming of the kingdom predicted by Jesus. In spite of their indeterminacy these two aspects of the predictions by Isaiah and Jesus establish the temporal boundaries of Mark's narrative world. Until some other coordinate is introduced to add a prior or subsequent moment, the narrative world is temporally closed. All other moments in the narrative world (story time), which includes those in the plotted narrative (plotted time), occur between these polar boundaries. But the poles also raise the further question of whether the time of Mark, his message, and his addressees is located between these poles or beyond them. From previous readings we may know the answer, and Mark's addressees would surely have known it too. But we do not know the answer from what has been disclosed in the narrative thus far and must therefore seek it from what is disclosed subsequently. Suffice it to say for now that chapter 13 locates the time of Mark's message before the coming of the kingdom and indicates that its coming is a major problem for Mark and his addressees. Even without this knowledge, however, it is a fact that the unfulfilled prediction about the kingdom introduces to the reader an element of *suspense* that will only be relieved when the question of when the kingdom will come is in some way addressed or answered. Thus far, therefore, the plot of the narrative has something to do with the coming of the kingdom proclaimed by Jesus.

The element of suspense is anchored in the plotting of certain coordinates. Plotted incidents being the description of successive actions by actors in the narrative sequence, the only plotted incidents in 1:1–15 are found in the descriptions of the appearances and activities of John and Jesus. Suspense enters this sequence in connection with the *predictions,* which prove to be the major *plot device* in Mark's narrative. Although predictions are issued in incidents that may or may not be plotted, what is predicted belongs to the level of story time until it comes to pass in the form of other plotted incidents. In this light, Isaiah's prediction was issued in an unplotted incident which therefore belongs to the level of story time. What he predicted in story time, on the other hand, is cited in the text in connection with its plotted fulfillment in the appearance and activity of the Baptist, which is the first plotted incident in the narrative. Similarly, John's prediction of one who would come after him occurs in the plotted incident in which he made it (1:7–8), while what he predicted is only momentarily an element of story time because it immediately comes to pass as a plotted incident in the form of Jesus' appearance and activity (1:9ff.). But when Jesus makes his prediction in the plotted incident of 1:14–15, what he predicts remains an indeterminate moment in story time until it comes to pass. Because his prediction is not fulfilled in 1:16ff., or anywhere else in Mark's narrative, the indeterminacy of its fulfillment creates the element of suspense. In 1:1–15 this suspense is heightened by the fact that three predictions are made but only two come to pass: Isaiah predicted something and John's appearance fulfilled it; John predicted something and Jesus' appearance fulfilled it; Jesus predicted something and . . . and what? That is the suspense, and it has been plotted by naming three predictors, three predictions, but only two fulfillments, the last of the three having been suspended. Suspense is therefore achieved by the unfulfilled prediction, and it is heightened because the expectation of its fulfillment is grounded in the two immediately preceding fulfillments. Schematically, the plotting looks like this:

story time

Isaiah's prediction   John's prediction   Jesus' prediction

plotted time

I indicated earlier that there is some question about whether the opening section of Mark ends in verse 13 or in verse 15. The use of predictions as a plot device offers some literary insights into this question. First, the scheme indicates that the text of 1:1–15 begins and ends indeterminately, on the one hand in the implied time when Isaiah issued his prophetic prediction, and on the other in the implied time when Jesus' prediction would be fulfilled. Thus the plotted action of the text begins with John fulfilling a prediction and making one of his own, which is also immediately fulfilled in the sequence of actions. Only John's action is completed in this section of text, and hereafter he ceases to be an actor. Second, John's narrative role is clearly subordinated to that of Jesus: by the content of his prediction, which refers to the coming of one who is mightier than he; by the descent of the Spirit upon Jesus (cf. 1:8) and by the voice that identifies him as its beloved son; and by Jesus' assertion that the time is fulfilled, presumably with the beginning of his preaching that the kingdom of God is at hand. In addition, because Jesus only begins this activity after John has been arrested, something new begins in 1:14–15, namely, the activity of Jesus, for Jesus is the principal actor or referent in all the incidents from 1:14 to the end of the text in 16:8. Indeed, from 1:14 on Jesus is also an actor in a different way from 1:1–13, where he is only a passive character (after he actively came to John). In 1:1–13 he is the one who was baptized by John, upon whom the Spirit descended, to whom the heavenly voice spoke, and who was driven by the Spirit into the wilderness where he was tempted by Satan and ministered unto by angels. In 1:14ff. he acts in relation to others. For all these reasons, verses 1–13 are different from 14–15 and the following narrative. Verses 1–13 introduce and 14–15 begin Jesus' activity in relation to the fulfillment of time which, having begun, is in a state of suspense until the kingdom of God fully comes. In 1:1–15 the reader is supplied with both information and expectations that give the reader a point of view—the narrator's—from which to construe what follows.

MARK 1:16—8:26

In view of the narrator's remarkable concentration on the plotting of temporal moments in 1:1–15, what follows it is striking. Unlike the fulfillment of the predictions by Isaiah and John, Jesus' prediction is not immediately fulfilled, and for a long time neither the kingdom nor other coordinate moments are referred to. Nor, for a long time, are other predictions made. Rather, there begins in 1:16ff. a sequence of episodes that temporally follow one after the other until the end of the narrative in 16:8. Beginning with Jesus' preaching in Galilee and ending with his resurrection from the dead, we have what looks like a biographical sequence of events concerned with a very narrow segment of the temporal continuum shaped by the coordinates of Mark's narrative world. Nevertheless, there is important evidence of temporal plotting, certainly after 8:27ff., when predictions again appear, but also before it. Let us pay our respects to this dividing line by concentrating first on 1:16—8:26. We may begin with a list of all references to events that occur before or after the incident (unit) in which the reference occurs, omitting those references that concern earlier or later moments *within* incidents (cf. 1:44; 5:19; 7:36).[4] In this way we will be able to honor

4. Also excluded from the list are summaries of what Jesus did over a period of time (e.g., 1:38–39, 45; 3:7–12; 4:34), or of responses to his deeds (e.g., 1:28, 32–34, 45, etc.).

the conclusion that Mark extensively used independent traditions while also showing how they have been poetically related to one another in the plotting of their relations. The letter *P* following textual references in the list indicates that the reference is to an earlier moment; all other textual references are to future moments.

References in 1:16—8:26 to prior or subsequent incidents

1:16–17	Jesus will make Simon and Andrew "fishers of men"
2:20	the bridegroom will be taken away and then the disciples will fast
3:2, 6	the Pharisees and Herodians seek a means of destroying Jesus
3:9	Jesus orders his disciples to prepare a boat for future use
3:14	Jesus appoints twelve followers "to be with him, and to be sent out to preach and have authority to cast out demons"
3:19	a reference to Judas Iscariot, who (subsequently) "betrayed" Jesus
3:27 (P)	a "strong man" identified with Satan (cf. 3:23ff.) was previously "bound"
3:28	all sins but one, blasphemy against the Holy Spirit, will be forgiven men
3:31–35 (P)	Jesus' past is implied by references to his home (3:19), his mother, and his brothers
4:11 (P)	the "secret of the kingdom of God" was previously given to the twelve and others (cf. 4:10)
4:12	forgiveness is a future possibility for some, but not for others
4:22	nothing is hid, except to be made manifest; nothing secret except to come to light
4:24–25	some will receive more than they have but others will have what they possess taken away
4:26–32	the kingdom is like something that begins small in size but ends up large, with both negative (4:26–29, harvest) and positive (4:30–32, nesting place) consequences

6:1–4 (P)	Jesus' past is implied in references to his own country, his mother, and his brothers and sisters
6:14–29 (P)	John the Baptist's execution is referred to as a past event
6:52 (P)	the disciples' failure to understand one incident (6:45–51) is explained as the consequence of their failure to understand the preceding incident (6:30–44)
7:6–13 (P)	past incidents of prophecy by Isaiah and of teaching by Moses ("the commandments of God") are referred to
8:12	no sign shall be given to this generation
8:17, 21 (P)	"Do you not yet perceive or understand," presuming a previous time from which understanding is expected
8:19 (P)	a past incident is explicitly referred to (cf. 6:30–44)
8:20 (P)	a past incident is explicitly referred to (cf. 8:1–10)

These references form a web of relations between incidents in Mark's narrative world. One kind of relation is reflected in those future references that anticipate moments which occur as plotted incidents later in the narrative, like Jesus' use of the boat in 4:1, Jesus the bridegroom being taken away in 14:1ff., the success of the authorities' conspiracy to destroy Jesus, also in 14:1ff., the sending of the twelve out to preach and exorcise in 6:7ff., and Judas's betrayal of Jesus, again in 14:1ff. Another kind of relation is reflected in the anticipation of things that do not come to pass by the time the narrative has ended, like Simon and Andrew becoming fishers of men, the forgiveness of sins, or lack of it, the making manifest of hidden or secret things, and the realization of the kingdom as harvest and as nesting place. Interestingly enough, all these seem to be related to the kingdom's coming or to things probably related to it. But even though they do not come to pass within the narrative, the fact that other future references or allusions do, only serves to heighten the expectation that they will too. We can therefore speak of such *anticipatory references* as a plot device closely related to that of predictions. In neither device is it necessary that the future moment is plotted, but because some are plotted as fulfillments both devices serve to create and reinforce narrative suspense.

References to past events are equally important because they have a retarding effect on the reader's progress through the narrative. At the moment when we come across new information about old things, whether plotted or not, we are required to pause, reflect, and assimilate, and then, at least mentally, work forward from the past incidents up to the one that created the pause, now with the new information and new understanding in mind. Thus the references to Jesus' home, country, and family supply information on the level of story, and we must "compute" its location in relation to the beginning of the narrative, for example, where it fits in relation to the beginning of John's and Jesus' activities. So it is also with the story-world information about Isaiah and now Moses, who is linked with the notion of the commandments of God, all of which belongs in the indeterminate past of Mark's narrative world. These examples, however, are far less significant for the poetics of Mark than the other past references in our list.

The reference to the strong man, that is, Satan, having been bound is in 3:20ff. connected with the narrator's idea that Jesus cast out demons with the aid of the Holy Spirit (cf. 3:29–30). Because exorcism is frequently referred to in 1:16—3:20 (cf. 1:21–28, 34, 40–45; 3:11–12, 15), 3:20ff. explains the power behind Jesus' activity as an exorcist, thereby providing information about what has happened previously in the narrative. But the demand for a pause by the reader is, rather, signaled by the notion that Satan was bound sometime earlier and by the reference to the Holy Spirit. For if the reader asks about when Satan was bound, the references to Jesus, the Spirit, and Satan lead him to associate these references with the previous occasion upon which he met them all, namely, in 1:12–13 in the incident concerning Jesus' temptation by Satan in the wilderness, where he was driven by the Spirit. If, as 3:27 tells us, demons can only be driven out after Satan has been bound, and if Jesus has been driving demons out since shortly after his temptation (cf. 1:21–28), which he must have overcome in order to have preached and cast out demons, then *within Mark's narrative world* the temptation incident in 1:12–13 is the occasion on which Satan was bound. Having drawn this conclusion the reader then rethinks and perhaps rereads 1:12—3:19 in its light. Now he knows what that business about exorcism was all about, although he now must also wonder about why Jesus prevented the exorcised demons from making his name known (cf. 1:25, 34; 3:11–12).

The same reading process is involved in 4:10–11, where we learn that some time previously the disciples had received the secret of the kingdom of God. On the one hand the reader is led to revise his understanding of the calling and commissioning of disciples in 1:16–20, 2:14, and 3:13–19, which are the only incidents in Mark's narrative world or plotted narrative in which Jesus might have given them the secret. On the other hand, the reader is also led back to the only previous reference to the kingdom of God, in 1:14–15. The last time he saw the notion of the kingdom he was left in suspense by it. Now he has to revise his understanding of it by realizing that already in the calling of the four disciples immediately after it the disciples were made a part of the suspense, which according to 4:10–11 has to do with the secret of the kingdom that Jesus made known to them, and to them alone (4:11–12). Perhaps, too, the silencing of the demons is related to the secret reserved for the disciples, since their silence prevents others, even the disciples, from knowing who Jesus was. Be this as it may for the moment, 4:10–11 links the suspense attending the future coming to the secret of it that the disciples and Jesus possess, but no one else, including, thus far, the reader, unless it refers to Jesus' identity as revealed by the demons. From 4:10–12 on the suspense about the kingdom is therefore suspense about the disciples' privileged knowledge of it, but also about their ignorance of Jesus' identity. The plot thickens.

Lest this kind of argumentation seem fanciful, as surely it must to traditional historical critics, let us hasten to observe that Mark unquestionably and self-consciously plots his narrative in such a way as to require the reader to do what we have just done. Of especial importance in this respect are the explicit backward references found in connection with the disciples in 6:52, 8:17 (cf. 8:21), 19, and 20, all of which, interestingly enough, are related to the question of the disciples' understanding raised by 4:10–12 (see also 4:13 and 7:18). In each case the reader is required to reflect back on previously plotted incidents in order to understand both them and what has transpired between them and the incidents in which the backward reference occurs. In each case the failure of the disciples to understand something in one incident is treated as the result of their failure to understand something in earlier incidents (see already 4:13). Consequently, corresponding to the diversion of suspense about the kingdom from Jesus to the disciples achieved in 4:10–12, we find that the plotting of incidents from 4:1—8:26 narrows this new focus by emphasizing the disciples' failure to understand the secret they have received—whatever that secret may be. Despite their privileged information they understand no more than others (cf. 4:10–13; 7:18). The poetic combination of the forward movement of episodes (heightened by anticipations of future episodes) with the backward references of some of them serve to involve the reader in a developing plot.

A final example of plotting that calls for our attention is the reference in 6:14–29 to the Baptist's death. This unit is of particular interest because it intrudes into the narrative in two ways, in one by introducing out of the blue Herod's view of who Jesus really was and in another by introducing a report of the Baptist's death that does not fit into the temporal sequence of plotted incidents in which it appears. Regardless of the intrusion of Herod, which as a plotted incident is "caused" by the preceding incident in 6:7–13 (cf. 6:14a), Herod (6:16) and the narrator (6:17ff.) refer to John's death as something that happened earlier, that is, in story time. Hence the disjuncture between story time and plotted time in the story of the Baptist's demise. But the importance of the disjuncture lies in the fact that it is for us a new example of a plotting device we may call *recollection*, that is, of past events in story time (cf. the related device of the flashback). Also belonging to this category are references to such things as the prophecies of Isaiah and the teachings of Moses, when they are not used in connection with the use of predictions as a plot device. That the report of the Baptist's demise is plotted and not merely the accidental result of the juxtaposition of sources is an issue whose answer leads to yet further insights into the poetics of Mark's narrative.

We cannot undertake here to provide all the reasons why this report is located where it is, or why Herod's intrusion should have occurred here and not elsewhere. There are, I think, both practical and structural reasons, but let us focus on the plotting device of *repetition* (cf. Jakobson's poetic function discussed above in Chapter II), which will prepare us to move on to 8:27ff.

In 6:14–16 the narrator tells us that three different guesses were being made about Jesus' real identity: that he was John the Baptist raised from the dead; that he was Elijah; and that he was "like one of the prophets of old." In 6:16 we are told that Herod favored the first option, following which the report of John's death is narrated. The same three guesses are cited once again in 8:27–29 when Jesus asks his disciples who people say he is. And once again the list is concluded when Peter responds to Jesus' question about who the disciples think he is by saying, "You are the Christ," that is Messiah or king (that kingship is referred to by "Christ" is indicated later in

15:32). The repetition thus elevates the problem of Jesus' identity and sets in opposition two alternatives: Jesus is the Baptist redivivus; Jesus is the king. But more is to come, for in 9:2–13 these relations are clarified. In 9:2–8 Jesus is seen by some of his disciples with Elijah and Moses, thereby ruling out any identification of Jesus with Elijah. But then, however, we find Jesus telling the disciples that Elijah *has come*, that "they did to him whatever they pleased" (9:13), and that now the Son of man will "suffer many things and be treated with contempt" (9:12). The sequence of Elijah and the Son of man corresponds to the sequence of John the Baptist and Jesus; John is construed as Elijah, Jesus as the Son of man. The Baptist suffered and died, as we learned in 6:17–29, and Jesus will suffer and die, as we will learn shortly. What I am suggesting is that the repetition seen in the triad of names in 6:14–16 and 8:27–29 extends into the references to the Baptist's death in 6:17–29 and 9:13 and, as we will see in a moment, that it does so in connection with Mark's further definition of temporal coordinates. Thus the plotting of the story of the Baptist's demise is based not on chronological sequence but on the information it provides about the relationship between Jesus' identity and John's. This relationship has a thematic status in Mark's narrative because it also appears in 1:1–15, 11:27–33, and possibly in coded form in the parable in 12:1–12.

MARK 8:27—10:52

Because 8:27—10:52 forms a segment by reason of its orientation to Jesus' three predictions of his fate as the Son of man, we can limit the next stage of our reflections to it. Temporally speaking, while past references proved especially important in 1:14—3:35 and 4:1—8:26, the three predictions of Jesus' passion, that is, of his death and resurrection, are symptoms of the striking future orientation of the incidents in 8:27—10:52. Regarding past moments we find two cases where an incident contains a reference to the one that precedes it (9:9 refers to 9:2–8 and 9:32 to 9:31), one where earlier stages of the narrative are referred to (10:28), and another in which we are told that the Son of man "came not to be served but to serve, and to give his life as a ransom for many" (10:45), thus putting the previously plotted incidents about Jesus in yet another light, one which shines as much, however, on the future incidents of his passion as on the past. Beyond these backward references Moses' story-time commandments are referred to twice (10:2–8, 19), and three times story-time events are alluded to as having taken place just before the incidents in which the allusions occur (9:17–18, 28; 9:33–34; 9:38). These few references notwithstanding, 8:27—10:52 supplies more information about the future temporal coordinates of Mark's narrative world than any previous segment, while also continuing the orientation of its plot to the disciples' lack of understanding.

The first future reference in 8:27ff. appears in the first of Jesus' predictions of his passion, that is, of his death and resurrection, in 8:31 (cf. 9:31 and 10:32–34). This prediction stands in temporal tension not only with the time of the incident in which it occurs but also with Peter's previous identification of Jesus in 8:29, "You are the Christ," that is, the king. The tension is created by the temporal opposition between what Peter says Jesus *is* and Jesus' prediction of his own future as the Son of man, which follows upon his suppression of the royal identity affirmed by Peter. Thus the suspense that attends any prediction is compounded by the plotting of the conceptual opposition between Christ and Son of man on a temporal axis. But before the reader can fully assimilate this new information about Jesus, including the new story-level coordinates represented by Jesus' future death and resurrection, further temporal information is provided in a speech by Jesus in 8:34—9:1. Here he speaks to his disciples and a crowd and links their behavior on the one hand to himself and his passion, and on the other to a future moment in which he will come as the Son of man "in the glory of his Father with the holy angels" to judge them for what they said about him and his words. And before this can be assimilated we find in 9:1 that the coming (or *parousia*, which transliterates the Greek word for "coming") of the Son of man is closely linked if not identified with the coming of the kingdom of God within the remaining lifetime of some who are present for the discourse, others by then having lost their lives for Jesus' sake and the gospel's. Happily, a much needed pause is called for in 9:2, where the narrator posits an interval of six or seven days between the incidents of 8:27—9:1 and 9:2 ff.

In 8:27—9:1 two future moments in story time are projected in two incidents in plotted time, and in each case tension is introduced that reinforces the suspense of the narrative. In the first projection we find a new tension between the plotted time understanding of Jesus as the king and the future coming to pass of a time when Jesus, as the Son of man, will be killed and then rise from the dead (8:27–31). The second projection is a little more complicated because it refers both to two points in time, the time of the plotted incident of Jesus' speech and the end time of Mark's narrative world, and to events transpiring between them (8:34—9:1). In the first case Jesus, who earlier identified himself as the Son of man who will die and rise, informs his audience that he will also come at the end-time as a judge (8:38; cf. 2:10). In the second case, he tells them that they must suffer and even die for his sake and the gospel's, and that he will judge them on the basis of their relationship with him up to the end (8:34—9:1). Taken together, the two temporal projections require the reader to revise further his previous understanding of Jesus as the proclaimer of the kingdom of God in terms of Jesus' passion and judgmental parousia as the Son of man. The effect of this revision is considerable.

For example, earlier we observed in connection with 1:14-15 that the initial suspense of the narrative was oriented to Jesus' proclamation of the kingdom and to the questions of when it will come and of how Jesus is related to it. These questions are now answered: Jesus is the Son of man who will die, rise from the dead, and return in judgment when the kingdom comes. And in 9:1 (see also 13:29-30), and as is presupposed in 8:34—9:1 as a whole (see also 10:15, 17-31), we now also learn an answer to the question of when the kingdom will come, namely, within the remaining lifetime of some of those present for Jesus' discourse! With this information the temporal closure, that is, the future pole of Mark's narrative world, is suddenly brought into a closer and determinate relationship with the plotted time of his narrative. As a result, the atmosphere of tension surrounding his plot is heightened at the same time that the suspense about when the kingdom will come and how Jesus is related to it is largely relieved.

A correlative effect of the new information in 8:27—9:1 concerns the disciples and their role in Mark's plot. Earlier we saw that 4:1 ff. introduces the disciples and their understanding of the secret of the kingdom into the plot and its suspense. The incidents in 8:27—9:1 serve to magnify the problem of the disciples and their impenetrable ignorance both by referring to it directly and by linking it to the suspense formerly associated with the question of Jesus and his relationship to the kingdom. The burden of suspense is therefore no sooner taken off of Jesus' shoulders than it is laid upon the disciples'. Let us examine more closely how this effect is achieved.

Mark 4:1—8:26 climaxes with Jesus' amazement that his disciples do not yet understand, but 8:27 ff. begins immediately with his candid questioning about their understanding of who he is, thereby establishing his identity as the locus of their problems. In the first incident (8:27–32a) they run through a list of popular conceptions to which they add their own: Jesus is the king. But Jesus charges them to tell no one about it and proceeds to teach them about his impending passion, calling himself "the Son of man." In the second incident (8:32b–33) Peter rebukes Jesus for his teaching, only to be rebuked in turn by Jesus, who calls him Satan and accuses him of thinking in terms of the things of men rather than of the things of God (this rendering better represents the Greek than, say, the RSV of 8:33 which in its reading of "being on the side of" lacks the key verb having to do with thinking and understanding, "phroneis"). Accordingly, thinking about Jesus as the king is to think about him in human terms, whereas thinking about him as the Son of man who must die and rise is to think of him in divine terms. With this distinction the plot of the narrative is redefined once more, now as the question of whether and when the disciples will come to think in divine terms and, whether they do or not, with what consequences. Thus far the only hint that they might succeed is implied by Jesus' persistence with them despite their deficiencies. His commitment appears to be anchored in the role he gave them as privileged sharers of his own role (cf. 3:13–15; 6:7–13, 30; 1:17), which occasions other problems in 10:35–45 (on which see below).

The third incident in 8:27—9:1 (8:34—9:1) obliquely refers back to the first two incidents while also pointing ahead to the end-time of Mark's narrative world. In it we learn that the disciples will also be subject to Jesus' end-time judgment, which some of them will live to see, and this threat suggests possible negative consequences for the disciples if they fail to come out of their cognitive slump. Indeed, the threat may even be more specific if the reference in 8:38, to those who are ashamed of Jesus and his words in this generation, is to the ignorant actions of the disciples in the second incident in 8:32b–33 (cf. 9:19). The likelihood of this reference is literarily supported by the fact that they are the only actors in the narrative context who are both followers of Jesus and ones who have just expressed "shame" about him (i.e., about his self-identification as Son of man rather than as king) and about his words (i.e., about his suppression of his kingship in favor of his impending passion). The "crowd" also present for Jesus' discourse (8:34a) does not share this experience, and their presence may only be a means of shaming the disciples by now openly ranking them with the crowds that do not share their privilege (cf. 4:10–13; 7:18; 8:14–21). Be this as it may, with the third incident in 8:27 ff. the reader learns that at the end-time Jesus will pronounce judgment even on his disciples and that some of them will have previously taken up their crosses for his sake and the gospel's, losing their lives in human terms but saving them in divine terms. Thus 8:34—9:1 concludes the opening section of 8:27 ff. by envisioning a continuous relationship between Jesus and his disciples right up to the end of story time. This implied lack of a radical break in their relationship has the further consequence of inclining the reader to emphasize the question not of whether but of when the disciples will come to understand things properly.

Following the pause between 9:1 and 2 ff. further temporal information is provided, not all of which is unambiguous. In 9:2–8 three disciples go off with Jesus and witness his transfiguration, which is accompanied both by appearances to them of Elijah and Moses conversing with Jesus and by a heavenly voice telling them that Jesus is its beloved Son (cf. 1:11), to whom they should listen (cf. the "words" referred to in 8:38, and Jesus' words in 8:30–33). The disciples seem not to have understood what they witnessed (cf. 9:5–6), but the only information provided about their experience is found in 9:9–10. There, following the incident in 9:2–8, Jesus charges "them to tell no one what they had seen, until the Son of man should have risen from the dead. So they kept the matter to themselves, questioning what the rising from the dead meant." The text continues in 9:11 with the disciples asking Jesus a question about something else, but we need to pause again to consider a new temporal coordinate introduced in 9:9. This coordinate also happens to provide the first concrete suggestion of a time when or by which the disciples may come to understand.

The new coordinate is the anticipated moment of a postresurrection time when the disciples are permitted to talk about what they have seen in the transfiguration. Although their ignorance is continued in their failure to understand "what the rising from the dead meant," the postresurrection moment is henceforth a part of the plotted suspense because it suspends the question of whether or not they will understand until it comes to pass. By introducing this relatively concrete moment to the reader's perception of his narrative's world, the narrator provides the first hint that the time of the disciples' ignorance will come to an end—after Jesus' resurrection from the dead. And by relating this moment to the fate of the Son of man, the narrator also identifies it with thinking in divine terms, thereby reinforcing the expectation that it will in fact come to pass. Needless to say, the disciples will have to understand what they saw before they can tell about it.

But what is the immediate literary significance of the transfiguration incident itself? Contextually, it is completely bound up with 9:9 as that about which the disciples should say nothing until after Jesus' resurrection, and because it can only be talked about later it too has an anticipatory function. Like all the predictions and anticipations, therefore, this incident functions for the reader, not for the actors, who do not understand it. For the reader, however, the incident also stands in tension with the incident in 1:11 when Jesus learned that he was the beloved Son, and with the incidents in which demons named Jesus as Son of God (cf. 3:11–12). In the plotted repetition of this information in 9:7 the reader learns that the disciples should have learned it from the transfiguration episode but did not. The story therefore reinforces yet again the opposition between thinking in human and divine terms. Nevertheless, unlike the many other indications of their ignorance this one opens out on the future because of the comment in 9:9 about the postresurrection moment. Thus the transfiguration story refers the reader both backward to the literary establishment of Jesus' identity in 1:11 (really 1:1–13), and forward to the disciples' realization of it after his resurrection, a not inappropriate literary function for an incident occurring almost at the midpoint of the narrative.

Yet there is an ambiguity in the transfiguration story when viewed in other than literary terms. Critics agree that it is anticipatory, but disagree about what it anticipates. Some say that it anticipates the parousia of the Son of man, viewing it in relation to 8:38—9:1, others that it anticipates a postresurrection appearance story not narrated in Mark, viewing it in relation to 9:9 on the one hand, and on the other in relation to an alleged postresurrection appearance story that appeared at the end of Mark's sources for his passion incidents, but which Mark relocated here. Source matters aside, our literary observations favor the second interpretation because a scene witnessed by only three disciples is hardly as public as the parousia, and because 9:9 presumes that the transfiguration will be understood and talked about only after the resurrection, if at all. Moreover, 9:9 does not give any indication of other incidents between Jesus' resurrection and this postresurrection moment. We will have to return to this issue later since subsequent temporal references produce the same differences of interpretation. For now, therefore, we need only keep our eyes open for references to postresurrection moments and the parousia.

The next incident in the opening section of 8:27 ff. adds to the remarkable temporal concentration seen thus far by dealing once again with end-time events. Apparently drawing on the end-time comments in 8:34—9:1 and on the reference to Elijah in 9:4 and 5, we find 9:11–13 addressing the subject of Elijah's coming before the end. Raising no little confusion about the appearance of Elijah in the transfiguration story, Jesus says that Elijah does come first, as the scribes say, but also that he *has* come, performed his task and been dispatched by others, and that now the Son of man "should suffer many things and be treated with contempt." Here Elijah is implicitly considered to be John the Baptist, while Jesus is the Son of man. Thus the end-time process has been introduced with the Baptist (see 1:2–8) and is now moving into its penultimate stage in the impending passion of Jesus. Then comes the end. When? According to 8:34—9:1, within what remains of the lifetime of Jesus' disciples. The end is less than a lifetime away.

In the incidents that follow 8:27—9:13, we find largely a repetition, with variation, of things seen in it. The disciples in various ways manage to perpetuate their ignorance and thereby fail to resolve the plot (cf. 9:14–29, 32, 33–50; 10:10, 13–16, 23–31). But the most important information comes in the intensification of certain issues in 10:32–45.

In the third and last prediction in 10:32–34 the suspense entailed in the previous two unfulfilled predictions is heightened when we learn (a) that Jesus and his followers are now on the way to Jerusalem, and (b) that it is in Jerusalem that the passion predictions will be fulfilled. As a result, the end of the penultimate stage, which is the Son of man's passion, is brought palpably near, and along with it the ultimate stage, that is, the coming of the Son of man and the kingdom. Equally important temporally is the related nearness of that postresurrection moment when the disciples might come to understand what they have yet to understand by the time of 10:32–34. Indeed, it is precisely their ignorance with which the section draws to a close in 10:35–45.

In 10:35–40 two disciples ask Jesus to let them sit on either side of him in his "glory." Jesus' first response is to tell them that they do not know what they are talking about, suggesting a gap between their understanding of his "glory" and his. But Jesus' response continues as he asks them whether they are able to drink the cup that he drinks or to be baptized with the baptism with which he is baptized. After they respond affirmatively, Jesus agrees that they *will* drink the same cup and be baptized with the same baptism, only to conclude that "to sit at my right hand or at my left is not mine to grant, but it is for those for whom it has been prepared" (10:39–40). Then he tells the twelve disciples that they must seek not to be rulers but rather to be slaves, "For the Son of man also came not to be served but to serve, and to give his life as a ransom for many" (10:41–45). The final incident in 10:46–52 refers to a man who calls Jesus "Son of David," which in 11:10 is associated with the royal kingship of the house of David that others saw coming with Jesus.

Mark 10:35–45 is reminiscent of 8:27—9:1. In each there is a tension between the time of the incident and an anticipated future time associated with Jesus. In each there is a reference to the behavior and fate of the disciples between these times. And in each the disciples misunderstand what Jesus is headed for, and in connection with a tension between the passion of Jesus as Son of man and his glory. The key notion in 10:35–45 is that of Jesus' glory, which the two disciples decide they want to share as they turn toward Jerusalem. Their decision is in part based on what they have already shared with Jesus, namely, the activity of preaching and exorcising, and in part on what they think Jesus' glory is. Jesus' response to their request is also reminiscent of 8:27—9:1 because it qualifies their expectations by interposing before his glory his passion and the passion of some of the disciples, which in chapter 10 is indicated both in the metaphors of the cup and of baptism and in the saying about the Son of man coming to serve and to give his life for others. But his response is also directly connected with 8:38 where Jesus associates his glory with the parousia of the Son of man "in the glory of his Father with the holy angels." Thus 8:38 also identifies "those for whom it has been prepared" (10:40) with the angels who will come with him at the end (see also 13:26–27). These links between the beginning and ending of 8:27—10:52 require us to see that the disciples' request to share in Jesus' glory entails their thinking about it in human terms, not the divine terms represented in the passion and parousia of the Son of man. But what are these human terms? Chapter 10 does not tell us, but the relations between it and 8:27—9:1 suggest that they had to do with the understanding of Jesus as a human king about to enter his royal glory in Jerusalem. And because the notion of the parousia of the

Son of man serves to interpret the meaning of the kingdom of God, just as the passion of the Son of man interprets Jesus' "kingship," it seems probable that the disciples construed Jesus' enthronement as the inauguration of the kingdom of God. The secret of the kingdom of God that the disciples failed to comprehend is therefore defined in terms of Jesus' identity as the Son of man who must die, rise, and return "in the glory of His father with the holy angels."

The possibility of the disciples' finally coming to grasp this secret is enhanced by the imminent passion of Jesus in which his predictions will be fulfilled, and by the anticipation of a moment after the passion when they will be able to talk about the transfiguration. In 8:27—10:52 the possibility is thematically reinforced by references to the disciples' experiences after the passion (cf. 8:34–37; 10:28–31; 10:39) and perhaps by the repeated references to their ongoing roles up to the end (cf. 8:34—9:1; 9:28–29, 33–37, 38–50; 10:10–12, 13–16, 23–27). It may be even a firmer possibility if we apply to the disciples' problem of understanding the solution posed by Jesus in 10:27: "with men it is impossible, but not with God; for all things are possible with God." Thinking in terms of the things of men, the overcoming of the disciples' ignorance is not very hopeful. But thinking in terms of the things of God is another matter, and it is our narrator who has told us so in the plotting of his narrative.

MARK 11:1—13:37

With the arrival of Jesus and his disciples in Jerusalem a new stage in the narrative begins. Although 10:32–34 leads the reader to expect the prompt fulfillment of the passion predictions, the moment of fulfillment is suspended for three (literary) days of incidents in which Jesus and the disciples go from Bethany (or the Mount of Olives) to the temple in Jerusalem, where Jesus teaches, and then back to Bethany (the relevant geographical and temporal indicators are in 11:1, 11, 12, 15, 19, 20, 27; 12:35; 13:1, 3). These days are separated from the days of the fulfillment of the passion predictions by the pause in 14:1–2. Nevertheless, with the beginning of daily reckoning in 11–13 the countdown for Jesus' last days begins.

The backward temporal references in 11:1—13:37 are again minimal. In 11:20–22 Peter remembers Jesus' cursing of a fig tree in a preceding incident (11:12–14), and in 11:30 and 32 there are references to the baptism of John. Besides these there are only story-time references to Moses, Abraham, Isaac, and Jacob (12:19

and 26; cf. 12:28–32). In the parable of 12:1–11 there are some oblique past references, but they are part of an allegorical story that encompasses the past, present, and future. Because the story refers to a "beloved son" who is killed, and to someone else killed before him, it is probable that these allude to the Baptist and Jesus. The thrust of the story is to the future, however, since it concludes with the destruction of the killers and the handing over to others of the land lent to them. Thus the story serves as a coded representation of some of the major coordinates in Mark's narrative world, a trait of parables in Mark (cf. 4:1–34).

The future orientation of these chapters is much stronger, although prior to chapter 13 there are only a few temporal references as the plotting is oriented to conflicts between Jesus and the authorities that will lead to the arrest of Jesus in chapter 14. In 11:1–10 Jesus enters Jerusalem, is hailed as one coming in the name of the Lord, and is associated with the coming of the kingdom of David (cf. 10:46–52; 12:35–37). But while his entry is depicted as being construed by some of the actors in royal terms, his presence in Jerusalem is viewed by the authorities as a threat to order that must be suppressed. Hence they conspire to seize him (cf. 11:18, 27–28; 12:12, 13). Shortly after Jesus' further teaching that the scribes "will receive the greater condemnation" (12:38–40), the activities of Jesus' last day of teaching in the temple come to a close with his prediction of the destruction of the temple (13:1–2). The last incident of the last day then takes place back in Bethany, at the Mount of Olives, where Peter, James, John, and Andrew, last seen as a foursome in 1:16–20, privately ask Jesus when the destruction of the temple will take place and with what advance signs (13:3–4).

Jesus' answer to this question takes the form of a lengthy address (comparable in length only with 4:1–34) in which he describes a number of events associated with the destruction of the temple, but goes beyond the question by relating the events to the end-time parousia of the Son of man (13:5–27) and by concluding with exhortations to watch for the previously described signs of the end, which will come within their lifetime (13:28–37; cf. 8:34—9:1). This apparent discrepancy between question and answer is bound up with Mark's plot (see already 8:27–31) insofar as all questions posed by the disciples to Jesus have up to now been thematically linked to the plot device of their ignorantly thinking in human terms (cf. 4:10–13, 38–41; 5:31–32; 7:17–18; 9:11–13, 28–29, 32; 10:10, 26–31, 35–40) and insofar as Jesus' comments about the Son of man (cf. 8:31 and 13:24–27) have been linked to thinking in terms of the things of God. Consequently, despite the lack of any mention about the disciples' understanding of Jesus' response, we are compelled to assume that they understood it no more than anything else. Thus the discourse functions principally in relation to the reader, supplying him with information the narrator wants him to have. This information must be examined accordingly, that is, as much in relation to the reader as to the disciples.

The information appears *not* to be presented sequentially, for Jesus' response begins in 13:5–8 with events that seem to be repeated in 13:19–23, making 13:9–18 refer to earlier events and 13:24–27 to later events. The earlier incidents deal with what we may call the disciples' mission to the nations (or gentiles), the central ones to events surrounding the destruction of the temple, and the later ones to the parousia of the Son of man. The issue at stake seems to be that in the future some people will interpret the central events as the time of the kingdom's coming, while Jesus (and the narrator) is saying, not yet, only afterward. Let us see.

In 13:5–8 we already find an important thread that runs throughout the discourse: Jesus consistently assumes that the four disciples to whom he is speaking will experience all the events he describes. This fact is underscored by his telling them that he has told them "all things beforehand" (13:23), and that "heaven and earth will pass away, but my words will not pass away" (13:31; cf. 9:7 and 8:38). The discourse makes no reference to a time when the disciples will overcome their ignorance, but these and other indications suggest that they will be representatives of Jesus up to the time of his parousia. We will return to these later.

Mark 13:5–8 begins Jesus' discourse with a warning that many will come in his name, saying, "I am he!" meaning either "I am the Christ" (cf. 13:6 and 14:62, in which RSV's "I am he" and "I am" render the same Greek words) or "I am Jesus" or both. Moreover, coming in Jesus' name means that these people are "Christians," and because they will try to lead the disciples and others astray divisions are presumed to emerge within the Christian community. The dividing line between the groups is created by believing or not believing the messianic claims made by some. According to Jesus and the narrator, these claims are false; neither the Christ nor Jesus has come, and "the end is not yet" (13:7). Thus, in the context of international warfare some will proclaim themselves to be the Christ (king) and the moment as the end, presumably meaning the kingdom of God because this "end" is later opposed to the parousia of the Son of man (13:26–27). As indicated earlier, the same errorists seem to appear again, but as the last stage in a sequence of events begun in 13:9ff. In 13:21–23 we read:

And then if any one says to you, "Look, here is the Christ!" or "Look, there he is!" do not believe it. False Christs and false prophets will arise and show signs and wonders, to lead astray, if possible, the elect. But take heed; I have told you all things beforehand.

Having arrived back at the starting point of the discourse, Jesus proceeds to describe the end, which we have seen to be the terminal coordinate in Mark's narrative world:

But in those days, after that tribulation, the sun will be darkened, and the moon will not give its light, and the stars will be falling from heaven, and the powers in the heavens will be shaken. And then they [the elect] will see the Son of man coming in clouds with great power and glory. And then he will send out the angels, and gather his elect from the four winds, from the ends of the earth to the ends of heaven. (13:24–27)

As noted above, the subsequent exhortations claim that the parousia will take place within the lifetime of the four disciples, confirming the proximity of the end otherwise suggested by the reference to its coming "in those days, after that tribulation" (13:24a).

Apart from the addition of the errorists and the warfare attending the destruction of the temple, the information about the parousia is the same as that seen in 8:38—9:1. The additions therefore serve as signs preceding the end. But the connections with 8:27 ff. are significantly more than this, for it was in 8:27–33 that we first saw Jesus called "the Christ" and in 8:34–37 that we first learned about the future suffering of the disciples for Jesus' sake and the gospel's. In 13:9–13 we find further information about the latter: at least the four disciples will not die, despite religious and political persecutions that will divide even families; the disciples' task will be to bear witness to Jesus as amidst persecution they preach the gospel to all nations (13:10); and when they are arrested and tried, the Holy Spirit will speak through them (13:11). And if they endure to the end, they will be saved. Let us note that the reference to the Holy Spirit speaking through the disciples may presuppose the story-time fulfillment of the Baptist's prediction that Jesus would baptize with the Holy Spirit (1:8), requiring us to envision besides a moment of postresurrection understanding and telling about the transfiguration, a baptism with the Holy Spirit, and, also, the commencement of the mission to the nations. A commencement of the mission must be posited somewhere in Mark's story world, and 13:11 is the only indication in Mark that the prediction of 1:8 might have come to pass in that world.

The remaining events projected in 13:14–20 concern the destruction of the temple, which is opaquely referred to in 13:14, which speaks of "the desolating sacrilege set up where it ought not to be," namely, in the temple. The reference is in scriptural code, the cipher to which is an earlier defilement of the temple described in Daniel 9:27, 11:31, and 12:11. At least one of the functions (metalingual) of the parenthetical "let the reader understand" (13:14) is to call attention to the coded reference to the temple. But another function may also well be to call attention to *events* of which the reader (addressee) is aware, thereby linking the time of Mark's writing to these events! Be this as it may for now, the defilement of the temple is an act of warfare that will lead to flight from Judea (locating the readers outside of Judea?) and into greater and greater tribulations, climaxing penultimately in the emergence of false Christs (kings) and false prophets. They will perform signs and wonders to lead the elect astray into believing that the end has come in connection with the events attending the destruction of the temple. If the reader is a participant in these events he must belong to the "elect" (13:20, 22, 27, and only here in Mark), who are in danger of being led astray. These, at least, are the only indications in Mark of the possible occasion for writing.

Finally, let us also file away for future reference the common sequence of three major points found in 8:27—9:1 and 13:5–27: (1) the identification of Jesus as the Christ, which in both cases is to some extent an erroneous perception of things in human terms; (2) the suffering of the disciples for Jesus' sake and the gospel's sometime before the end, and therefore after the time of Jesus' passion; and (3) the reference to the parousia of the Son of man as the proper understanding of the coming of the kingdom, which in both texts is defined as coming within the lifetime of some of the disciples. Given these relationships, it is striking that in 8:27–33 it is the disciples who are in error, whereas in chapter 13 they are defenders of the truth against others guilty of their own previous error of pointing to someone as the Christ. In each case, therefore, we see depicted a conflict of interpretations, on the one hand of who Jesus was, and on the other of whether the events surrounding the destruction of the temple signal the end.[5] Throughout, the position of Jesus and the narrator, which defines the point of view of

---

5. Note that signs and wonders are interpreted as end-time indicators in 3:20–30, 8:11–12, and 13:23, and that Jesus' disciples performed them too (cf. 3:16; 6:7, 13; 9:14–29).

the narrative, is constant, only the position of the disciples changes—in time and with the introduction of new "actors" who take the position formerly held by them. Surely in this complex of relations are the clues to the time of writing and the meaning of Mark's message.

MARK 14:1—16:8

Before we look at the backward and forward references in this section we must observe one fact about it that is of fundamental importance for the plotting of Mark's narrative: In 14:1—16:8 the plotted incidents are based on the fulfillment of the three sets of passion predictions seen in 8:27—10:52, and of the related anticipations of Jesus' death and resurrection. The significance of this seemingly trivial observation—trivial because it is self-evident—is that the fulfilled predictions systematically confirm the reader's narrator-controlled expectation that Jesus' predictions will ineluctably come to pass. Jesus' "words will not pass away" (13:31). He has told the disciples "all things beforehand" (13:23). What is more, the effect of this confirmation of expectations is to lead the reader to believe that all Jesus' other predictions and anticipatory utterances will also come to pass, despite the fact that Mark's narrative concludes with the fulfillment of only the passion predictions. Therefore, when the reader concludes the narrative he does so with the full expectation that while plotted time has come to an end, story time has not. Mark's narrative concludes like a novel that ends before the inevitable resolution of its plot because the novelist has made the resolution appear inevitable. Unlike such novels, however, the historical reference of Mark's narrative supplies real-world information to the original addressees, whereas we are methodologically limited to the relationship between the narrative world and the plotting of it. Our literary approach reveals information about the real world only to the extent that we can infer it from the narrative itself (as for example in chapter 13). Beyond such inferences we cannot go without extrinsic information such as might come from other texts. Our results therefore require external corroboration but only, I believe, after the other texts have been approached in the same way. So let us avoid the referential fallacy as we continue our way through to the end of the narrative, keeping in mind the relationship between its end and the story-world events that occur between it and the end-time of the story-world itself.

Backward references to earlier incidents are found in 14:49, which refers to the daily teaching in the temple seen in 11:1—13:37; 14:72 describes Peter's remembrance of Jesus' words to him in 14:30; and 16:7 refers to Jesus' words in 14:28. More general references appear in 14:58, where false witnesses claim that Jesus said he would destroy the temple; in 15:39, where a centurion says that Jesus was (or had been) a son of God; and in 15:40–41, which refers to women who had been following Jesus since Galilee.

Before turning to the future references we should observe some predictions made in 14:1—16:8 that are also fulfilled in it, for these only reinforce the expectation of fulfillment. In 14:8 Jesus' body is anointed even before he dies in chapter 15; in 14:1–2 and 10–11 Judas and the authorities conspire to arrest Jesus, and do so in 14:43ff.; in 14:12–16 Jesus tells the disciples what they will find in Jerusalem, and they "found it as he had told them" (14:16; cf. 11:2–6); in 14:18 Jesus predicts that one of those present will betray him, and he does in 14:43ff.; and in 14:29 Peter says he will not abandon Jesus, but does in 14:66–72, while in 14:31 the others say the same, but in 14:50 forsake him and flee when he is arrested. One significant consequence of the flight of the eleven and of the defection of the twelfth is that by 14:72 the twelve cease to be actors in the plotted incidents of the narrative. The plot of the narrative is therefore suspended in yet another way: the flight of the disciples, which is their climactic act of ignorance, is accompanied by their removal from the narrative's action. How will the problem of their ignorance be resolved if they are not present? Mark has, as we will see, an answer to this question.

The future references other than those fulfilled in the narrative of course refer to story time. Some of these are less striking than others. For example, Jesus refers in 14:9 to the preaching of the gospel in the whole world, which we have seen previously in 13:10, and in 14:25 he speaks of not drinking again of the fruit of the vine until he does so in the kingdom of God, which at best hints only at the nearness of the kingdom. More significant than these are his predictions in 14:62 and in 14:27–28, the latter of which is referred to again in 16:7 and very much concerns the resolution of Mark's plot. Let us consider first 14:61–62.

In 14:61 the high priest before whom Jesus has been brought asks him: "Are you the Christ, the Son of the Blessed?" Jesus answers in 14:62: "I am; and you will see the Son of man seated at the right hand of Power, and coming with the clouds of heaven."

Construing this as blasphemy, the high priest and other authorities turn Jesus over to Pilate who has Jesus executed as "the king of the Jews," "the Christ, the king of Israel." Consequences aside, the reader knows that the priest's question and Jesus' answer refer to two different ways of looking at things, the human and the divine. Like the questions and answers in 4:10–12 (cf. 4:13ff.), 8:27–31, and 13:3–37, Jesus' response goes beyond the question, showing that for Jesus (and the narrator) the answer is the important thing, not the question. In this case Jesus accepts the priest's interrogative identification of him as "the Christ, the Son of the Blessed," but goes beyond affirming it to qualify it in terms of the Son of man, as he did in 8:27–31. But now that his passion is fully in progress (since 14:43) he does not refer to the passion of the Son of man, but to future moments, one of which is new. While we have seen references to the Son of man coming with the clouds of heaven at the end (8:38—9:1; 13:26–27), we have not previously seen mention of his being seated at the right hand of Power, although 9:1 speaks of the kingdom coming with power, and 13:26 of the parousia of the Son of man with great power and glory. Only the rejected request of the two disciples to sit beside Jesus in his glory may be related to this new moment, and that negatively since Jesus opposed their notion of his glory with one like that referred to here (cf. 10:35–40).

The new coordinate established by Jesus' reference to the Son of man being seated at the right hand of Power is of interest for our understanding of Mark's narrative world because it answers the reader's potential question of where Jesus, the Son of man, will be between his passion and his parousia. Jesus' response to the high priest identifies three periods in Jesus' career as the Son of man: (1) his time as a character whose actions are plotted in the narrative, namely, the time of the passion of the Son of man (cf. the Greek of 9:31, and 10:45); (2) the time after it when he will be seated at the right hand of Power until (3) the time of his parousia at the end, when the kingdom, properly understood in relation to the Son of man, will come. Accordingly, while worldly events in Mark's story time will continue until the end, Jesus will be seated in heaven. Mark does not tell us by what means Jesus ascended to this place, or when, but it must be located shortly after the completion of his passion. Mark 14:61–62 therefore adds yet another story time incident to the immediate postresurrection time.

Closely related to this problematical postresurrection time is the complex of predictions in 14:27–30, one of which is referred to again in 16:7 just before the narrative ends. Shortly before Jesus' arrest he tells the twelve disciples:

"You will all fall away; for it is written, 'I will strike the shepherd, and the sheep will be scattered.' But after I am raised up, I will go before you to Galilee." Peter said to him, "Even though they all fall away, I will not." And Jesus said to him, "Truly, I say to you, this very night, before the cock crows twice, you will deny me three times." But he said vehemently, "If I must die with you, I will not deny you." And they all said the same.

There are essentially three predictions contained in this message— the predictions of Jesus' arrest, of the flight of the disciples, and of Jesus going before the disciples to Galilee after his resurrection. We have already considered those that come to pass as plotted incidents, namely, all but the journey to Galilee. And we have already seen that these fulfillments result in the absence of the disciples from the narrative after 14:72, leaving suspended the question of when they would overcome their ignorance. Yet intruding into this suspense-full question is now the suspense attending the one unfulfilled prediction of Jesus going before the disciples to Galilee after his resurrection. Since the passion predictions and all those in 14:27–30 but this one come to pass in the plotted incidents of 14:1—16:8, the reader is compelled to balance in his mind *two* questions: When will the disciples overcome their ignorance, which is climaxed by their abandoning of Jesus? And what is this projected meeting in Galilee all about? In the balance, these two questions become one: What is the relationship between the meeting in Galilee and the unresolved plot of Mark's narrative?

Should the reader have failed to conceive these questions, the narrator encourages him to do so once again when, at the very place where a postresurrection incident might be expected, he describes an incident in which the reader is explicitly reminded of the unfulfilled prediction. When a number of women went to Jesus' tomb to anoint his body, they encountered an open tomb and a "young man" who addressed them as follows:

Do not be amazed; you seek Jesus of Nazareth, who was crucified. He has risen, he is not here; see the place where they laid him. But go, tell his disciples and Peter that he is going before you [i.e., them] to Galilee; there you [i.e., they] will see him, as he told you. (16:6–7)

The evidence of plotting in this incident is threefold: (1) in the uniquely self-conscious backward reference to what Jesus told the disciples in 14:27–28; (2) in the forward reference to a (story) time immediately after the resurrection, seen previously only in 9:9 after the transfiguration incident earlier seen to be anticipatory; and (3) in the anticipatory reinsertion into the story time of the disciples, who have been absent in plotted time since 14:72 but have been reintroduced in connection with their seeing Jesus in Galilee, where he has gone ahead of them. At no point in any of this evidence is any incident contemplated between the passion of the Son of man and his meeting with the disciples in Galilee. In all cases it is described as following immediately after the resurrection.

The narrator has by these means unequivocally directed the reader to relate the disciples, still beclouded by ignorance, to the impending story-time incident in Galilee. By doing this principally through the use of an unfulfilled prediction, he also brings to bear on this anticipated moment the whole weight of his major plot device of prediction and fulfillment. Precisely because so many predictions have come to pass in plotted time, including the fulfillment of the passion predictions and others in 14:1—16:8, the reader cannot doubt that all of those yet to be fulfilled by the end of plotted time will be fulfilled in story time. The meeting in Galilee is the first of these, and it is the prerequisite for others: for the overcoming of the disciples' ignorance and the resolution of the plot of Mark's narrative; for the baptism of the disciples with the Holy Spirit, which is presumably prerequisite to their undertaking the mission of preaching the gospel to all nations; and for the seating (enthronement?) of the Son of man at the right hand of Power. Thus the meeting in Galilee cannot be the parousia of the Son of man, as many critics have supposed. In addition to the prediction and fulfillment sequence in 14:1—16:8, there stand against that supposition also the immediate postresurrection signals in 9:2–10 and the signs in Mark 13 that well before the end the disciples, or at least four of them, will have abandoned their position of ignorance only to find it taken up by errorists. The projected meeting in Galilee is the only moment of all those in Mark's narrative world when the disciples could come out from under the cloud of ignorance—when the plot of Mark's narrative could be resolved.

Finally, we come to the one potential stumbling block for our literary conclusions: in the last words of the narrative we find that the women who had been directed to report to the disciples fled from the tomb and said nothing to anyone (16:8)! Read apart from the literary insights we have gained, we could conclude from this that because the disciples never learned of Jesus' resurrection or of the meeting in Galilee the plot of Mark's narrative is either unresolved or resolved negatively. Since the historical conclusion following from this reading of 16:8 leads to the view that Mark wrote to reject totally the historical disciples of Jesus,[6] the literary evidence must be carefully assessed. The evidence is basically the same as that for seeing the meeting in Galilee as a postresurrection moment in which Mark's plot *was* resolved shortly after Jesus' resurrection. To it we can add that in the plotting of the entire narrative what Jesus says comes to pass despite the understanding and deeds of the disciples. God's terms supersede men's. The best example of this is 14:27–30, to which the verse before 16:8 explicitly refers. The "scattering of the sheep" refers to incidents superseded by Jesus' prediction of the meeting in Galilee, as we can see in the words of the "young man" to the women at the empty tomb. The flight of the disciples is simply disregarded in the reminder about Jesus going on to Galilee, where the disciples would see him. Indeed, since all but Jesus, the narrator, and the reader stand under a cloud of ignorance until Galilee, the fearful flight of the women is no more determinative of what Jesus will make happen than Judas's betrayal, the flight of the ten, and Peter's default on his promise. The flight of the women belongs to the scattering of the sheep. The last words of the narrative may refer to thinking and acting in human terms, but these are not the last things in Mark's narrative world, which in the last analysis is determined by divine terms. The silence of the women is broken by Jesus' words, which "will not pass away" (13:31).

CONCLUSION

We have seen that Mark's narrative world is temporally bounded on the one hand by an indeterminate past and on the other by a future moment that becomes increasingly determinate in the course of the narrative's plotting. This future moment—the parousia of the Son of man—is in every sense the end of Mark's narrative world, because it signals the termination of that world's previous social order and the goal toward which that world's history was directed. In relation to this end-time our intrinsic literary considerations have produced three rather striking pieces of information: (1) the plot of the narrative is oriented to the suspense

---

6. See T. J. Weeden, *Mark: Traditions in Conflict* (Philadelphia: Fortress Press, 1971).

attending the disciples' ignorance of Jesus' identity and therefore of his role in the end-time process; this plot is resolved not in the narrative itself but outside of it in connection with a projected postresurrection meeting between Jesus and his disciples in Galilee; (2) among the many story-time events projected in the narrative, the narrator is most concerned with one that some people who are not actors in the narrative will falsely interpret as the end, and in so doing seek to lead four disciples and the elect astray; (3) the first two points intersect because the ignorant (human terms) understanding of the disciples prior to the meeting in Galilee is the same one as that to be taken by the false interpreters and deceivers just prior to the real end-time. This intersection between plotted events and projected events, together with the four disciples' reversal of positions, raises the literary question of how Mark's long story about Jesus' disciples is related to the errorists' later threat to them and to the elect. The only literary answer is that the disciples' change of position—their coming to the position of Jesus and the narrator—reveals that the errorists are doubly wrong, wrong in fact, as Mark 13 shows, and wrong because repudiated by the four disciples who, having formerly held the erroneous position, came to abandon it. In supplying this answer, however, much more is implied, namely, that the disciples have some position of authority in that later time, an authority which would make their "conversion" a weighty argument against the errorists. But with this conclusion we find that our literary answers lead to historical questions. Indeed, to make sense of our literary answers we need to answer the principal historical question of why Mark told his addressees all of these things.

I think the literary relationship between the disciples and the errorists is bound up with the nonfictional nature of Mark's narrative—that unlike fiction its narrative world corresponds to the narrator's and addressees' real world. Regardless of how accurately the narrative world corresponds to that real world, the perceptions of the correspondence shared by the addresser and the addressees supply the missing link in our understanding of Mark's message. At this juncture, therefore, we have to draw some historical inferences from the poetic evidence we have seen.

Given the nearness of the end-time and the focus of Mark 13 on threats to the elect in the time shortly before the end, we must agree with many critics that the occasion for Mark's writing is in the time just before the end projected by Mark, namely, in the time of the errorists. Since the narrative is *about* the disciples, they are not the addressees, leaving only the elect as possible candidates for this role. Mark the addresser therefore sends his narrative message about Jesus' disciples to his addressees, the elect. The addressees, victimized by errorists who take a certain position, find in the message that the disciples, four of whom may be with the elect or honored by them if not, formerly took the same position as the errorists. The message confirms for the elect that this position is erroneous by showing that Jesus repudiated it in his time, that the disciples repudiated it in a postresurrection meeting in Galilee, and that Jesus predicted the reemergence of the position in the form of the errorists' penultimate end-time activity. Yet the question remains: What necessitates the narrative form of a story about the disciples when other forms of repudiation would have served equally well, as Paul's letters show, as the Apocalypse of John shows, and as the apologetic and antiheresiological writings of the second century show? I suggest that the necessity of narrative form can only be accounted for if the historical errorists of Mark's time and the elect's were locating the authority of their message in stories about Jesus' teachings to his disciples. On this basis we can see that Mark's strangely negative and extensive picture of the disciples in the time of Jesus functions not merely to repudiate the errorists but also to undercut systematically the authority that they claimed from some of the disciples by showing that the disciples themselves once held an erroneous view but later abandoned it. At least the four disciples of Mark 13 are reclaimed for the elect. The literary and historical focal point of Mark's case is the postresurrection meeting between Jesus and (some of) his disciples in Galilee. Literarily, this is the moment when Mark's plot was resolved; historically, this is the moment that socially and theologically distinguishes the elect from the errorists.

These few conclusions follow from the intrinsic poetics of Mark's narrative. While they have intruded into the realm of historical reconstruction, that extrinsic critical task remains to be completed in connection with internal discrepancies in Mark (e.g., Jesus and the disciples preach repentance, but Jesus teaches in a form designed to preclude it; cf. 4:10–12), and in connection with other texts. Questions of sources, redaction, and genre can now be asked in a new light, however, since literary criticism presents the historical critic not only with a bona fide narrative but also with literary-critical insights that may help him better to understand old problems at the same time that they introduce new ones.

IV

Narrative World and Real World in Luke-Acts

A long-standing issue in Pauline studies concerns the evidential value of Luke's narrative for reconstructing the history and thought of Paul. The issue arises because of differences between what Luke says about him in Acts and what he says in his own letters.[1] Since Paul's letters are a primary source for the events in which he participated, and Luke's comments about him only a secondary source, the evidential priority of the letters is axiomatic in the historical-critical tradition. But Luke's comments are also potentially useful because he refers to many things Paul does not write about. The problem is to know when Luke can be relied upon and when he cannot. One criterion frequently employed in making such decisions is literary in fact if not in name. If, for example, the speeches of actors in Acts all look alike in their form and theological content, and if the thoughts Paul expresses in his letters are not represented in the speeches Luke attributes to him, then the speeches in Acts are considered literary (redactional) creations and for this reason unreliable as evidence for what Paul said. As literary creations they are rather evidence for what Luke thought and for what he was saying to his addressees in communicating with them through his narrative. Literary insights have therefore served historians both with regard to the positive evi-

1. For discussion and literature see Werner G. Kümmel, *Introduction to the New Testament*, rev. Eng. ed. (Nashville: Abingdon Press), pp. 151–88, 250–55. See also his chapter on Luke's Gospel for further background to issues raised in this chapter, and W. Ward Gasque, *A History of the Criticism of the Acts of the Apostles* (Grand Rapids: Eerdmans, 1975), on the history of research. Charles H. Talbert, "Shifting Sands: The Recent Study of the Gospel of Luke," *Interpretation* 30 (1976): 381–95, addresses current issues.

dential value of Luke's narrative for understanding his time and to its negative value for understanding the events to which it refers.

I referred in Chapter I to these evidential aspects in connection with two corresponding analytical principles followed by historical critics. In Chapter III we explored the first principle in our consideration of the evidential value of Mark's narrative for understanding the time when he wrote it. In this chapter I want to take up the second principle in order to illustrate the contribution of literary insights to the historical problem of reconstructing the events to which a text refers. Recalling our discussion of the referential fallacy in Chapter II, we will focus on the plotting of Luke's narrative world in order to avoid confusing it with the real world. Since the narrative world of Luke-Acts is a full one indeed, for purposes of this case study we can select a single historical issue and consider the literary evidence pertinent to it.

The issue I have in mind is one rarely dealt with by historical critics, yet it is one that bears fundamentally on our understanding of Paul and the early history of Christianity. The issue concerns Luke's description of Paul as a missionary who in every town went first into Jewish synagogues to preach to Jews and then turned to gentiles only after segments of his Jewish audiences had forced him to leave their synagogues, and often their towns, trying on occasion even to kill him (see Acts 13—28). Luke's description is historically questionable because from Paul's letters we learn three things that contradict it: (1) Paul understood his Damascus-road experience as a commission to preach to the gentiles, not to Jews, and this was confirmed some years later by James and Peter (cf. Gal. 1–2 and Acts 15); (2) in the periods for which Acts and Paul provide overlapping information, Paul only talks about his work with the gentiles and repeatedly stresses the polarity between (Christian) Jews and gentiles in his understanding of his mission, in which the gospel proceeds from (Christian) Jews to gentiles, and in his understanding of the collection, which reciprocally proceeds from the gentiles to the (Christian) Jews (cf. Gal. 2:7–10; 1 Cor. 16; 2 Cor. 8; 9; Rom. 9—11; 15:7–33); Acts makes no mention of the collection from the gentiles, which according to Romans 15 was the occasion for Paul's final trip to Jerusalem described in Acts 19:21 ff.; and (3) Paul *never* refers to his having preached in Jewish synagogues or, therefore, to his going to gentiles only after being rejected by Jews; indeed, the word "synagogue" never occurs in Paul's letters.

Having stated the contradiction between the two accounts, Paul's comments now serve as independent primary-source evidence for real-world events to which Luke refers. Should our examination of the plotting of Luke's narrative world prove that his description of these events is integral to the distinctive plotting of his narrative, his description of them will become evidence for understanding his message at the same time that it ceases to be evidence for Paul.

Although we have narrowed our focus to incidents related to Paul, the evidence bearing on them is found throughout Luke-Acts. According to Luke, Paul was not the only one rejected by Jews in connection with his preaching in their sanctuaries; Jesus, Peter and John, and Stephen all had the same "experience." Virtually the whole of Luke's narrative world and a considerable part of its plotting therefore bear on the incidents in which Paul is involved, and they do so in two ways. On the one hand, as a narrative Luke-Acts begins at one point in time and moves through a sequence of episodes to another point in time. The plotted repetition of certain kinds of episodes—let us call them rejection incidents—comprises one aspect of Luke's art as a narrator. On the other hand, however, critics have long recognized that Luke's Gospel and Acts are parallel compositions![2] In what follows I want to show that in both the sequential and parallel aspects of Luke's composition *the rejection of God's agents by God's people in connection with God's sanctuaries (synagogues and temple) is the plot device by which the movement of the narrative as a whole is motivated.*

THE PARALLEL COMPOSITION OF LUKE'S GOSPEL AND ACTS

We may begin with the aspect of parallel composition because it offers some methodological controls that enable us to establish a position rather quickly. The controls derive from the very close relations between Luke's Gospel and the Gospels of Matthew and Mark. Usually these relations are discussed in terms of sources and redaction, since it is widely believed that Luke and Matthew used Mark's narrative as a source. Our concern, however, is not with the way Luke redacted his sources but with the way he has composed his narrative. From this perspective the relations that are

2. See especially A. J. Mattill, Jr., "The Jesus-Paul Parallels and the Purpose of Luke-Acts: H. H. Evans Reconsidered," *Novum Testamentum* 17 (1975): 15–46, and for these and other parallels, Charles H. Talbert, *Literary Patterns, Theological Themes and the Genre of Luke-Acts*, SBLMS 20 (Missoula: Society of Biblical Literature and Scholars Press, 1974).

of interest are the *differences* between Luke and the other two narratives, for the differences raise the question of whether *they* perform any distinctive functions in the composition of Luke's two-volume narrative. For example, Luke's Gospel differs from the others by having an extensive section devoted to Jesus' journey to Jerusalem (Luke 9:51—19:44), and this difference is paralleled by an equivalent journey in Acts, where Paul makes a similar decision to journey to Jerusalem, and does so (Acts 19:21—21:16). Together, the difference between Luke and the other Gospels and the relationship between it and equivalent sections in Acts raises the question of the literary function of these journeys in Luke-Acts. Methodologically, the perception of differences is facilitated by reading Matthew, Mark, and Luke in a Gospel Parallels and by the use of a concordance to check the distinctiveness of Luke's vocabulary (e.g., his use of travel language and references to the temple, synagogues, and cities). In the following chart I presume the use of this comparative method and of these tools. The chart represents the results of a comparative study. The middle column contains a list of successive sections in Luke's Gospel, the right-hand column a list of corresponding sections in Acts, and the left-hand column a succession of verbal statements describing the actions of these sections in terms of their functions within each volume.

Parallel Relations Between the Gospel and Acts

ACTIONS	LUKE	ACTS
Preparation of the actor(s) culminating in their baptism with the Holy Spirit	1:1—4:13	1:1—2:4 (or 2:47)
His resultant ministry in Jewish sanctuaries and in cities, constituting confrontations between the actor and the people of God	4:14—9:50	2:5 (or 3:1)—19:20
Ministry subordinated to his journey to Jerusalem and his fate there	9:51—19:44	19:21—21:16
His activity in the temple, again constituting a confrontation	19:45—21:38	21:17-26

Legal proceedings taken by the Jewish authorities against him, constituting a rejection of his ministry (a "passion" episode)	22:1—23:49	21:27—26:32
God's reaffirmation of him and of his own plan, extending beyond established Judaism	23:50—24:53	27:1—28:31

This chart represents no parallels that have not been previously observed by other commentators, although some differences obtain in the number of sections and in the location of their boundaries in terms of chapter and verse references.[3] What is new in it is rather its representation of the organic unity of the sections and of their narrative functions within their respective volumes. The individual incidents in each section of each volume form functional sections of narrative in which each section is oriented to a different kind of action related to the central actor. Collectively, the several sections represent what Aristotle called a complete action. Thus the individual incidents are single actions that belong to sections of narrative, each of which is characterized by a certain kind of action, while the sections taken together represent a single action, a complete whole. Luke's Gospel therefore represents the complete activity of Jesus, as construed by Luke, and Acts represents the equivalently complete activity of the twelve apostles and Paul, the collective "actor" of Acts when viewed as a parallel composition to Luke's Gospel. Each volume's total action thus constitutes a story. But what are these stories? In each case the story concerns the confrontation between an accredited agent of God and the people of God in their sanctuaries (synagogues and temple), with the confrontation climaxing in the legal rejection of the agents by the official representatives of the people of God, which is in turn followed by God's reaffirmation of his agents and by the extension of God's plans beyond his traditional people and holy places to others. In the Gospel the other people are the apostles and those who followed Jesus (cf. Luke 24); in Acts they are the apostle Paul and

3. See Mattill, "The Jesus-Paul Parallels and the Purpose of Luke-Acts"; Talbert, *Literary Patterns, Theological Themes and the Genre of Luke-Acts*; and Kümmel, *Introduction to the New Testament*, on Luke and Acts.

the gentiles to whom alone he brings the gospel (cf. Acts 28). In both volumes the new places of God are the places in which his growing new "people" gather. In light of the parallel composition of Luke's Gospel and Acts we must view these volumes as two parallel "actions." On the other hand, the sequential composition of Luke-Acts requires us also to view Luke-Acts as a single action! More can therefore be said about the parallel sections in the course of our consideration of the sequential axis of Luke's narrative.

THE SEQUENTIAL COMPOSITION OF LUKE-ACTS

Our chart of the parallel sections in Luke and Acts discloses in each volume two separate sections oriented to confrontations between the agents of God and the people of God in their sanctuaries. In each volume the first of these sections is conspicuously differentiated from the section immediately following it because in the former the agents repeatedly enter cities and sanctuaries (Luke 4:14—9:50; Acts 2:5/3:1—19:20) while in the latter they are passing through cities and towns on their way to Jerusalem (Luke 9:51—19:49; Acts 19:21—21:16; cf. the one exception vis-à-vis synagogues in Luke 13:10–21 and 13:22). In each volume, these journey-sections are followed by the second segments in which the agents of God are active in sanctuaries, and in each case in the temple at Jerusalem (Luke 19:45—21:38; Acts 21:17–26). This activity leads to their arrest and trial (Luke 22:1—23:49; Acts 21:27—26:32), which is followed by concluding sections describing God's reaffirmation of his agents and the extension of God's will into the future, apart from his people of old (Luke 23:50—24:53; Acts 27:1—28:31). In order to see how these sections are related to one another in the sequential composition of Luke-Acts, let us encode them as follows: P = the preparation of the actor; S^1 = the initial activity of confrontation in sanctuaries; $\longrightarrow$ = the journey to Jerusalem; S^2 = the terminal confrontation activity in the temple; R = the trial in which the actor is rejected; and $\Longrightarrow$ = God's reaffirmation of the agents and the forward movement (extension) entailed in it. Accordingly, the parallel composition of Luke and Acts can be represented as:

$$P/S^1 \longrightarrow S^2/R/ \Longrightarrow$$
$$P/S^1 \longrightarrow S^2/R/ \Longrightarrow$$

Sequentially, the several sections can be described continuously:

$$P/S^1 \longrightarrow S^2/R/ \Longrightarrow P/S^1 \longrightarrow S^2/R/ \Longrightarrow$$

To this scheme we need to make some additions that will help us to see further aspects of Luke's sequential plotting. The first addition concerns a third arrest and trial found in Luke's account of Stephen in Acts 6—8. As other critics have observed, this account is literarily equivalent (or parallel) to the "passions" of Jesus and Paul.[4] Unlike the other legal hearings found twice in Acts 3—5 and once in Acts 18, these three trial episodes or passion stories are described as the final resolution of matters by the Jewish authorities: Jesus is executed according to their demand; Stephen is stoned to death by them; and Paul is saved from their hands and sent by Romans to Rome for the final settlement of the case against him. Besides these relations, however, Acts 6—8 further breaks the parallel pattern of composition, in which it occurs in S^1, by having its own concluding extension component (8:1-3). After Jesus' execution the narrator points to the disciples and their future baptism with the Holy Spirit that will empower them to undertake a mission to the gentiles. After Stephen's execution the mission to the gentiles begins with the scattering of all but the apostles throughout the region of Judea and Samaria (cf. Acts 1:8) and with the references to Paul; gentiles begin to enter the church in 8:4ff. And finally, after Paul's arrival in Rome the gospel is preached to the gentiles only. Thus the "passions" of these three actors mark progressive stages in the sequential plotting of the antagonism between the agents of God and the people of God. The plot of Luke-Acts is bound up with the incidents in which the narrator represents this antagonism, and it is resolved when in Acts 28 Paul breaks the structure of antagonism by ceasing to go to the Jews, preaching henceforth only to gentiles. With the final incident in Acts 28 the antagonism comes to an end, and so does Luke's narrative. Luke-Acts is therefore literarily complete, and no projected or lost third volume is called for, as many critics have done. This means, too, that Luke's message is concerned with the way in which his plot is resolved, namely, with the movement of God's agents beyond Jewry as a result of its persistent rejection of the word of God brought by his agents. And because a new people of God is formed in the process of this movement (let us call them "Christian"; cf. Acts 11:26; 26:28; and also 15:14) the message of Luke-Acts concerns the disengagement of Christianity from Judaism, that is, the process by

•

4. See F. Foakes Jackson, "Stephen's Speech in Acts," *Journal of Biblical Literature* 49 (1930), pp. 283–86; and Robert Morgenthaler, *Die lukanische Geschichtsschreibung als Zeugnis*, pt. 1 (Zurich: Zwingli Verlag), pp. 159–94.

which Christianity became "a religion distinct from Judaism" (Haenchen).[5]

By creating a sequence of three major rejection incidents, the episode concerning Stephen enables us to break through Luke's pattern of parallel composition to his sequential plotting. Further insights into sequential composition are afforded by another class of individual incidents representing the antagonism between the agents of God and the people of God. Also breaking the pattern of parallel composition, this class of incidents is nevertheless related in two ways to the confrontations in sanctuaries earlier represented by the sigla S^1 and S^2. On the one hand there are six confrontation incidents located in sanctuaries (see below), two of them appearing before each of the three rejection incidents. We can therefore in a preliminary way identify a relationship between this pattern of distribution and that seen in Luke's scheme of parallel composition: in both systems S^1 and S^2 are followed by R. On the other hand, each of the six confrontation stories is internally structured in a manner closely corresponding to this same fundamental scheme. Our concern for Luke's sequential composition is best served by exploring first the sequential distribution of these six incidents. In order to see the relationship between their distribution and the distribution of sections in our scheme of Luke's parallel composition, some minor revisions of our earlier sigla are necessary. Thus we can drop the P element, which functions principally if not solely in the system of parallel composition; we can read the S elements as individual incidents rather than as sections comprised of many incidents; we can read the arrow ⟶ as representing not a journey but rather the narrative distance between the two S incidents; and we can retain the R and ⟹ sigla to refer to the rejection and extension elements, remembering that on the axis of sequential composition there are three of these. With these revisions we can describe the plotted sequential distribution of incidents representing the antagonism between the agents of God and the people of God in the following way:

$$S^1 \longrightarrow S^2/R/\Longrightarrow \quad S^1 \longrightarrow S^2/R/\Longrightarrow \quad S^1 \longrightarrow S^2/R/\Longrightarrow$$

As we will see, because the confrontation *incidents* (S) contain their own internal rejection (R) and extension ($\Longrightarrow$) elements,

---

5. Ernst Haenchen, *The Acts of the Apostles: A Commentary*, trans. Bernard Noble and Gerald Shinn (Philadelphia: Westminster Press, 1971), pp. 539–40.

they combine with the rejection and extension incidents to provide the dynamic, causal motivation for the progress of Luke's two-volume narrative. These divisions are not static boundary markers between literary units.

The six confrontation incidents are found in Luke 4:16–30, 20:1–19; Acts 3—4, 5:12–42; and Acts 13:13–52, 18:1–11. Let us remember that these incidents occur in the larger sections seen in the parallel composition of the Gospel and Acts, but also that on the level of sequential composition they are not bound to parallel relations between the two volumes. Indeed, only the rejection and extension elements at the end of the Gospel and Acts function in both the parallel and sequential compositional systems! Two questions now arise: On what basis can we say that these six incidents are significantly different from other incidents in Luke-Acts and at the same time significantly related to one another? Although the answer to the second question is a partial answer to the first one, our observations will be tidier if we deal with the questions separately.

Critics have long recognized distinctive differences in all six incidents. Luke 4:16–30 is universally acknowledged to be distinctively Lukan because it differs in location, form, and content from the parallel material in Matthew and Mark (cf. Matt. 13:54–58; Mark 6:1–6), and Luke 20:1–19 is in setting, structure, and content also recognizably different from their versions of it. (Cf. Matt. 21:10—22:14; Mark 11:15—12:12; and Luke 19:45—20:19.) Similarly, Acts 5:12–42 has long been seen to be repetitious of Acts 3—4, and the content of Acts 13:13–52 is widely recognized as being reiterated in 18:1–11 (and again in 28:17–31 which, however, is not located in a sanctuary like our six incidents). Thus the distinctiveness of our confrontation incidents is widely acknowledged, as are the relations between the two sets of incidents in Acts. Admittedly, the distinctiveness is *not* spoken of in terms of differences between them and other stories in Luke-Acts, although that is implied in the recognition of their peculiar features. Admittedly, too, the relations between the six stories is not recognized, and neither is the relationship between the two sets of incidents in Acts and the rejection (trial) incidents that follow them. Yet it is self-evident that the two incidents in Acts 3—5 are followed by the story of Stephen and that the incidents in Acts 13:13–52 and 18:1–11 are literarily related to Paul's arrest and trials (R) in Acts. Equally self-evident is the relationship between the conspiracy theme found in Luke 4:16–30 and 20:1–19 and the success of the conspirators in the story of Jesus' arrest, trial, and execution.

These general considerations suggest that our six stories are distinctively different from other stories in Luke-Acts, but exactly how they differ, and with what effect, can only be seen by observing the relations that obtain between them. For them to belong to the plot device of equivalence (or repetition or parallelism), these relations must be established.

If we begin with the most obvious features these stories have in common, it is immediately apparent that they all contain confrontations in sanctuaries between agents of God and the people of God and that they all contain overt rejections of the agents' activities by the people or the authorities. Each of the six stories therefore contains both S and R elements. Importantly, no other stories in Luke-Acts contain both these features in a single incident. Only the summary accounts in Acts 14:1–7 and 17:10–15, and the extended story in 17:1–10, come close, but not to the point of being shaped by the confrontation and rejection elements. But our six incidents share yet other features that further distinguish them from other stories and more closely relate them to the pattern we have been tracing. Each story also contains an extension element ($\Longrightarrow$) following the rejection, and each also evidences another distinctive feature, namely, an interruption of the agent's action that divides it into two parts corresponding to the previously observed twin confrontations, S^1 and S^2. The interruption functions as the audience's response to the opening action, while the closing action responds to their interruption. Before we define these features more closely, let us revise our sigla once again in order to account for the similarities and differences between the internal structure of our six incidents and the parallel and sequential systems we have already considered. First, since the confrontation in the sanctuary is divided into two parts let us use the lower case s to represent the two parts, s^1 and s^2. Second, let us now use the arrow $\longrightarrow$ to represent the interruption which leads to s^2. Third, recognizing that the rejection elements are not final legal solutions but thematically related to them as anticipations of them, let us use the lower case r to represent this element. And finally, as suggested above, we can retain our sign $\Longrightarrow$ for the extension elements. With these revisions each episode can be described with our now familiar formula: $s^1 \longrightarrow s^2/r/\Longrightarrow$. For purposes of comparison another chart will serve to define the relations between the six episodes.

LUKE 4	LUKE 20	ACTS 3–4	ACTS 5	ACTS 13	ACTS 18
s^1 4:16–21	20:1/9–16a	3:1–10	5:12–16	13:13/16b–42	18:5/1–5
⟶ 4:22	20:16b	3:11	5:17–20	13:43–45	18:6a
s^2 4:23–27	20:17–18	3:12–26	5:21	13:46–47	18:6b
r 4:28–29	20:19	4:1–22	5:22–40	13:48–50	(18:12–17)
⟹ 4:30	(20:19ff.)	4:23–31/37	5:41–42	13:51–52	18:7–11

To develop the argument for these relations further would require more detailed discussion than we can or need entertain here.
Despite the differences between each of these episodes, the relations
suggested by the chart can be defended at almost every point, while
no other episodes in Luke-Acts are shaped like them. Only Luke
13:10–17 comes close, because of the interruption in 13:14. But this
unit not only lacks a rejection element, it also extends beyond 13:17
to 13:21; for Luke 13:10–21 comprises a single incident, thereby
distinguishing it from our six units. On the other hand, the
similarities between them and Luke 13 raise a new subject for
another inquiry, namely, the thematic elements associated with
them.

CONCLUSION

Beyond the often cited parallelisms in Luke-Acts lies the Jakobsonian principle of equivalence as a plot device by which the
"message" poetically refers the reader to itself. Because of the
historiographical pretensions of Luke as a narrator, the poetic and
referential functions of his message stand in tension with one
another. That the referential world projected by his message does
not correspond with the real world has been suggested by the
extrinsic testimony to this world supplied by Paul. This conclusion
is strongly supported by intrinsic poetic evidence which reveals that
Luke's description of Paul's activities is integrally bound up with
probably his principal plot device of repeated confrontation and
rejection incidents. We have found this device in three aspects of
Luke's plotting: in parallel composition; in sequential composition;
and in the composition of six strategically plotted individual incidents.

Our literary explorations have centered on the narrative world of
certain texts. In the case of Mark's narrative we have explored
the plotting of this world and its implications for our understanding of his message to his addressees. In the case of Luke-Acts, we

have explored the relationship between his narrative world and the real world, and discovered that the plotting of the former deepens the gap between it and the real world. The lesson of both case studies is that the literary criticism we have employed serves best and directly the first principle of historical criticism by supplying us with information about the time of writing. If this conclusion seems negative with regard to the referential concerns embodied in the second principle, we should perhaps remember that the historian must use many methods and that literary criticism is but one of them. Yet even in its negative implications, it has produced positive results—by lending greater weight, for example, to the better evidence supplied by Paul and by offering new literary evidence to the redaction and source critics who wish to gain access to the earlier evidence found in the sources underlying our present texts.